T0170721

Pox, Empire, Shackles, and Hides

Pox, Empire, Shackles, and Hides

The Townsend Site, 1670–1715

JON BERNARD MARCOUX

The University of Alabama Press
Tuscaloosa

Copyright © 2010
The University of Alabama Press
Tuscaloosa, Alabama 35487-0380
All rights reserved
Manufactured in the United States of America

Typeface: Berkeley Oldstyle

∞

The paper on which this book is printed meets the minimum requirements of
American National Standard for Information Sciences-Permanence of Paper for
Printed Library Materials, ANSI Z39.48-1984.

Library of Congress Cataloging-in-Publication Data

Marcoux, Jon Bernard.
    Pox, empire, shackles, and hides : the Townsend site, 1670–1715 / Jon Bernard
Marcoux.
        p. cm.
    Includes bibliographical references and index.
    ISBN 978-0-8173-1716-4 (cloth : alk. paper) — ISBN 978-0-8173-5628-6
(pbk. : alk. paper) — ISBN 978-0-8173-8483-8 (electronic) 1. Cherokee Indians—
Tennessee—Townsend—History. 2. Cherokee Indians—Antiquities. 3. Cherokee
Indians—Dwellings—Tennessee—Townsend. 4. Households—Tennessee—
Townsend—History. 5. Excavations (Archaeology)—Tennessee—Townsend. 6.
Townsend (Tenn.)—Antiquities. I. Title.
    E99.C5M3398   2010
    975.004′97557—dc22
                                                                            2010017117

For Christine

Contents

Illustrations

TABLES

Acknowledgments

A number of individuals helped to make this book a reality. To begin with, I thank Brett Riggs for sharing with me his encyclopedic knowledge of Cherokee written and oral history and archaeology, his wit, and his encouragement. I also thank Vin Steponaitis, Brian Billman, Margie Scarry, and John Scarry for mentoring me for eight years. I am fortunate to have access to such brilliant and genuine people.

While a graduate student at UNC-Chapel Hill, I was part of a cadre of students pursuing similar research interests, and the cross-pollination of insights among these folks led to many of the ideas that appear in the following pages. These colleagues include Greg Wilson, Tony Boudreaux, Amber VanDerwarker, Chris Rodning, Jennifer Ringberg, Lance Greene, Julio Rucabado-Yong, Mark Plane, Barker Fariss, Ben Shields, Erik Johannesson, Erin Grantham, and Drew Kenworthy.

My study was supported by the Tennessee Department of Transportation's (TDOT) Townsend Archaeological Project and administered through the Archaeological Research Laboratories (ARL) at the University of Tennessee. I am grateful to Boyce Driscoll of the ARL and Gerald Kline of TDOT for allowing me to participate in the Townsend Archaeological Project and for giving me the freedom to pursue my research interests. While I was working at the ARL facilities in Knoxville, Cameron Howell and Rachel Black went out of their way to provide me with any information I needed. I am also indebted to Kenneth Cornett for generously sharing his knowledge of the archaeology of the Little River valley.

My project also benefited from the offer of data and assistance from a number of researchers and research institutions. I am indebted to Patricia

Nietfeld and Tom Evans at the National Museum of the American Indian and James Krakker at the Smithsonian Institution for their time and help with glass trade bead collections. I thank Steve Davis for allowing me full access to the glass trade bead collections and database at the University of North Carolina's Research Laboratories of Archaeology (RLA). I am grateful to Jane Eastman for providing glass trade bead data from her dissertation as well as for conducting the analysis that resulted in the glass bead data in the RLA database. Christopher Rodning also generously offered unpublished data from his dissertation. I thank Gerald Schroedl for allowing me to incorporate data from his U.S. Forest Service–funded excavations at the site of Chattooga.

As with most people who choose this vocation, I am most fortunate to have an incredibly supportive and understanding family. I thank my mother Jean Marcoux for her love of education and a lifetime of encouragement and support. Lastly, I thank my wife Christine Campbell Marcoux, who without a doubt is the very personification of serendipity.

1

Introduction

Returning from a diplomatic mission to the Overhill Cherokee towns in 1762, a regiment of Virginia colonial infantry marched through the western reaches of the Appalachian Mountains along what is known as the Great Indian Warpath. Upon reaching the Little River near present-day Maryville, Tennessee, the expedition leader, Lieutenant Henry Timberlake, commented, "At this place had formerly been an Indian Town, called Elajoy (Ellejoy); and I am surprised how the natives should ever abandon so beautiful and fertile a spot. Were it a more polished country, it would make the finest situation for a gentleman's seat I ever saw" (Timberlake 2001 [1762]:118–119). Indeed, why would the Indian group living in this town permanently abandon its community? The historical record is virtually mute when it comes to this mystery. Nineteenth-century historian James G. M. Ramsey (1999 [1853]:88) is the only other remotely contemporaneous source to mention the town of Ellejoy, which he calls Allejay. Ramsey offers no further information about the town, but he states that there were a number of additional communities in the vicinity called the Tuckaleechee Towns. As the moniker implies, these towns were located in present-day Tuckaleechee Cove just upriver from Ellejoy. The inhabitants of these communities were doubtless Cherokee, but the towns were located some 50 km north of the Little Tennessee River valley—the region typically attributed to eighteenth-century Cherokee settlements. The absence of these towns in period censuses and maps suggests that they were abandoned decades before Timberlake's march, during a period of time known as the English Contact period (ca. 1670–1715). That the abandonment of these communities occurred at this time is not surprising, for this was a very unsettled period for southeastern Indian communities, most of which were weathering the widespread effects of disease, slave raiding, warfare, and large-scale population displacements.

In this study, I take up the deceptively simple mystery pondered by Timberlake; however, instead of solely asking why the inhabitants of the Tuckaleechee Towns abandoned their communities, I also explore the reasons these remote towns were settled in the first place and what daily life was like for the members of local households. In the absence of documentary evidence, I rely on the methods and theoretical frameworks of anthropological archaeology to develop interpretations of daily life within these communities. I utilize the Townsend site, which contains three archaeological sites (40Bt89–40Bt91) that represent part of a Tuckaleechee Towns community, as a case study to examine the strategies that households enacted while adapting to the social, political, and economic turmoil that followed European contact.

RECONSIDERING THE ENGLISH CONTACT PERIOD

We cannot begin to answer questions about daily life in the Tuckaleechee Towns without first considering the historical context of the period in which community members were living. Being marked by disease, warfare, and massive population displacements, the English Contact period (ca. 1670–1715) was an extremely turbulent time for the Cherokee and for other southeastern Indian groups. Written history, however, often belies the dynamic character of this period. Indeed, seminal southeastern histories present the late seventeenth and early eighteenth centuries as part of a singular grand narrative couched in the teleological language of Indian passivity, technological dependence, and the inevitability of European dominance (e.g., Corkran 1967; Crane 2004; Reid 1976; Swanton 1998).

More recently, historians and archaeologists have replaced this grand narrative with the notion that "history" is made up of the highly variable and exceedingly local outcomes of interaction among native groups and Europeans (Bowne 2005; Ethridge 2006; Gallay 2002; Galloway 2002; Martin 1994; Oatis 2004; Ramsey 2001; Wesson 2008). In their historical narratives of the English Contact period, the social, economic, and political landscape that emerges is highly unstable. Some of the authors use the theoretical concept of the *shatter zone* to describe the landscape of disruption that resulted from the clash of global European trading systems with local "traditional" southeastern Indian societies (e.g., Esarey 2007; Ethridge 2006). All of the authors stress the agency of small groups, particularly households and individual communities, and their ability to negotiate the turmoil of the period through strategic action. In a sense, they are following the call of historian John Phillip Reid (1976:117), who decades earlier presaged, "We will never know the Cherokee [or other Indian groups] until we hear from these lesser individuals: the nonheadmen, the warriors, hunters, farmers, and traders [I would add women also] who did not negotiate or played secondary roles in negotiations with the Europeans." In this study, I ask the following question: How would a narrative of daily life during the English Contact period read for the everyday folk living in the households of the Tuckaleechee Towns?

When viewed from this perspective, the question of why individuals settled and abandoned the Tuckaleechee Towns becomes a much more complex problem, for the answers can only be found through an in-depth analysis of the playing out of the various strategies that constituted daily life in Cherokee households amid the sweeping social, political, and economic changes of the late seventeenth and early eighteenth centuries. The location of a community in the regional landscape, local community history, the spatial distribution of households within a community, architecture, and even the pottery that was made and used by community members all become crucial components of strategic actions taken by households on a daily basis in order to adapt to life in the English Contact period. In this way the members of the Tuckaleechee Towns were hardly passive recipients of history but rather active participants in it (Wesson 2008).

English Contact Period Cherokee Communities at a Glance

The Cherokee first enter into European history in the late seventeenth and early eighteenth centuries through the writings of English traders, travelers, and diplomats. Beginning with these first encounters, the act of defining *Cherokee* became an ongoing process of identity creation for both groups. For purposes of introduction, we must begin with a necessarily rough cultural sketch. By the first decades of the eighteenth century the Cherokee were settled in 60–65 politically independent communities each inhabited by 100–600 people (Schroedl 2000; Smith 1979). These communities were distributed on the southern Appalachian landscape in three main settlement clusters that corresponded to socially recognized divisions among the Cherokee. The three divisions included the Lower Settlements in present-day northeastern Georgia and northwestern South Carolina; the Middle, Valley, and Out Town settlements in western North Carolina; and the Overhill or Upper settlements in eastern Tennessee. Differences in spoken dialect and pottery manufacture have convinced scholars that these settlement divisions had considerable time depth (Bates 1986; Egloff 1967; Gilbert 1943;

Mooney 1900; Riggs and Rodning 2002; Schroedl 1986). Within these clusters, settlement types consisted of large nucleated towns, small hamlets, and dispersed individual farmsteads.

Cherokee communities engaged in horticulture including the classic North American triumvirate of cultigens (corn, beans, and squash), supplemented by hunting and gathering wild foods. European-introduced plants (e.g., peaches and apples) and animals (e.g., pigs, cattle, chickens) made up a much smaller portion of the diet and did not play a significant dietary role until the latter half of the eighteenth century (Bogan et al. 1986; Schroedl 2000; VanDerwarker and Detwiler 2000, 2002; Walker 1995). Eighteenth-century ethnohistoric descriptions and early twentieth-century ethnological research indicate that the Cherokee were also divided into seven exogamous matrilineal clans. Status differences among members of Cherokee communities were much less pronounced than in communities of the preceding Mississippian period (ca. A.D. 1000–1600) (Rodning 2004). Historical evidence demonstrates that the power of most Cherokee leaders was primarily based on charisma, persuasion, and achievement and was largely confined to the community level. Furthermore, political decision making on both the community and supracommunity level was a matter of consensus among councils rather than edicts of a single ruler (Gearing 1962; Gilbert 1943).

English, French, and Spanish documents tell us very little about how late seventeenth- and early eighteenth-century Cherokee communities were affected by disease, slave raiding, warfare, and population movements; however, there can be little doubt that these communities felt their disruptive effects. For example, although there is no written record of the effects of a 1696 smallpox epidemic among the Cherokee, Peter Wood (1989:63) estimates that they might have lost half of their population, shrinking from 32,000 in 1685 to 16,000 by 1700. The 1708 and 1715 colonial censuses indicate that the Cherokee population continued to decline after the epidemic (although at a much lower rate) to 11,000. Gallay (2002:298–299, Table 2) laments the lack of any historic records quantifying the number of Cherokee slaves taken between 1670 and 1715, but his estimate places the number in the hundreds if not at a thousand—a relatively low number compared with other groups. Scant archaeological evidence and oral tradition suggest that by the time the first South Carolina traders arrived in the mountains in 1690, the Upper Cherokee were in the process of adjusting to population losses by shifting their settlements—abandoning their settlements north of the Little Tennessee Valley and consolidating their population into established towns along the Little Tennessee and Hiwassee rivers to the southeast (Ethridge 2006:211; Hudson 2002:xxxiv; Rodning 2002).

THE ARCHAEOLOGY OF CHEROKEE COMMUNITIES

The fields of history and ethnohistory have done much to reconstruct the cultural and political landscape experienced by Cherokee communities during the English Contact period. As greatly improved as this reconstruction is, however, it has necessarily been rendered in broad strokes by the physical and cultural constraints imposed by the historical (i.e., written) record. In order to transcend the interpretive bonds of this "paper cage," we must search for alternative sources of knowledge. Among these sources, the archaeological record has shown much promise (e.g., Dickens 1976; Riggs 1999; Rodning 2002, 2004; Schroedl 2000; Schroedl, ed. 1986). Indeed, by virtue of its disciplinary focus on material culture rather than written records, archaeology has enabled Cherokee researchers to explore lines of inquiry that have complemented those followed by historians. Two fundamental research questions have long been at the center of Cherokee archaeology: (1) What are the prehistoric and/or protohistoric "origins" of the Cherokee? and (2) How have change and stability played out in Cherokee culture in the face of sustained European interaction? (see also Dickens 1979, Rodning 2004, and Schroedl 2000 for additional syntheses of past research).

Research Addressing Cherokee "Origins"

Scholarly interest in the archaeology of the Cherokee began with a focus on ancestry. The earliest excavations were carried out by the privately funded Valentine Museum and the Smithsonian Institution's Division of Mound Exploration as part of the (in)famous mound-builder debate of the last decade of the nineteenth century (Dickens 1979; Schroedl 2000; Thomas 1894). These excavations took place at sites within the documented eighteenth-century Cherokee homeland in western North Carolina with the goal of determining whether the earthen mounds that dotted this mountain landscape were the handiwork of Cherokee ancestors or were the constructs of folk with a more mythical pedigree (e.g., a lost tribe of Israel). After many trial excavations, continuity in various forms of material culture, most notably pottery, could not be ignored and the researchers concluded that the earthen mounds were indeed wholly indigenous phenomena.

The notion of a Cherokee origin for the earthen mounds and artifacts found throughout the southern Appalachian region was reinforced by the ethnographic and ethnohistoric reconstructions of James Mooney (1889, 1900). The historical portrait Mooney painted featured the Cherokee breaking away from linguistically related northern Iroquois groups and migrating southward just prior to European contact in the sixteenth century. This interpretation guided major museum-funded excavations undertaken in the early twentieth century. Motivated by an urgent desire to salvage a history for the "disappearing" Cherokee and armed with a zeal to amass a worthy collection of artifacts with which to trace out that history, members of the Heye Foundation's Museum of the American Indian undertook a number of mound explorations in North Carolina and Georgia during the early twentieth century (Heye 1919; Heye et al. 1918; Turbyfill 1927).

In western North Carolina, Heye Foundation excavations were conducted at the Garden Creek site in Haywood County (Heye 1919; Keel 1976) and at an unnamed mound site located along the Notley River in Cherokee County (Turbyfill 1927). Results of the excavations at the Garden Creek site were published in a small pamphlet (Heye 1919). The results of the excavations of the Notley River mound were never formally published. The only mention of the site exists in a two-page typewritten report on file in the National Museum of the American Indian archives (Turbyfill 1927). The Heye Foundation excavations in northeast Georgia were focused on the Nacoochee mound in White County. While by no means exemplary by modern standards, the reporting of these excavations was definitely more thorough (Heye et al. 1918). Indeed, the written descriptions of the excavations and the illustrations of material culture in the 1918 report rivaled those of works produced by the Smithsonian's Bureau of American Ethnology decades later. In all of these Heye Foundation projects, Cherokee affiliation was taken as a given, and pottery and earthworks were described as "typical Cherokee" (Heye 1919:36; Heye et al. 1918:103). Heye and his colleagues, however, had no sense of the temporal depth represented by the artifacts recovered from these sites, which we now know were occupied for centuries before European contact (Riggs and Rodning 2002; Rodning 2004).

Archaeological syntheses necessitated by the massive Depression-era public-works projects of the 1930s provided later researchers with a greatly improved understanding of southeastern culture history and its time depth. One of the major contributions of this era was the establishment of broad regional and supraregional cultural chronologies based on material culture trait lists (e.g., McKern 1939, 1943; Webb 1939; Webb and DeJarnette 1942). While now dismissed as arcane "essentialist" frameworks (Lyman et al. 1997), these lists were truly revolutionary in that they enabled researchers to make empirical intraregional and interregional comparisons with archaeological data. In the South Appalachian region, the use of trait-list comparisons led researchers to differing conclusions regarding Cherokee origins.

The 1933 Smithsonian Institution excavations at the Peachtree site in the upper Hiwassee River valley uncovered a platform mound surrounded by the remains of a village. In the report of excavations, Frank Setzler and Jesse Jennings (1941:6–13) specifically framed their research around testing the hypothesis that the site was "Cherokee in origin." They stated that historical records did not locate a Cherokee village in the area, but the presence of glass trade beads and other diagnostic eighteenth-century European artifacts in burial contexts indicated that a Cherokee group occupied the site at some point during the historic period. The authors compared a variety of material culture traits from the Peachtree site to those of other sites in the region, including attributes related to the earthen mound, burial forms, and a myriad of artifact types. They found a combination of material traits related to what were defined at the time as "Woodland" and "Mississippi" cultures, but they stopped short of concluding that the site represented a continuous occupation by the Cherokee and their ancestors, saying, "we would hesitate to label the component as pure Cherokee, or even to assign it unequivocally to any linguistic or ethnic group" (Setzler and Jennings 1941:57). Thus, while the authors speculated that a Cherokee group occupied the site in the eighteenth century, their admitted lack of understanding of occupational time depth resulted in a necessarily ambiguous conclusion regarding the earlier (and more substantial) occupations at the Peachtree site. Nevertheless, Setzler and Jennings moved Cherokee archaeology forward by demonstrating the need for empirical comparison in constructing any (pre)history for the Cherokee.

Relying on similar trait-list comparisons among sites in East Tennessee, Lewis and Kneberg (1946; Lewis et al. 1995) offered a provocative interpretation of Overhill Cherokee origins in this region. In their published report of excavations at the Hiwassee Island site in the upper Tennessee River valley, they (Lewis and Kneberg 1946) highlighted the presence of a number of burial traits that did not appear to be typical for eighteenth-century Cherokee communities. Certain interments contained late seventeenth- and early eighteenth-century European artifacts, but historic accounts did not place any Cherokee towns in the vicinity of Hiwassee Island during this period. Also, most of the burials were secondary inhumations, a form not typically associated with historic Cherokee groups (Lewis and Kneberg 1946:132–135). Furthermore, two of the burials contained plain shell-tempered pottery vessels that were stylistically different from the paddle-stamped pottery typically associated with Cherokee groups to the east. Combining these pieces of evidence with other data from their trait list, the authors argued that the burials at Hiwassee Island were definitely not Cherokee; instead, they believed that the burials represented the last vestiges of a local Muskogee-speaking Mississippian community (Lewis and Kneberg 1946:15). They further argued that the Iroquoian-speaking Cherokee were an intrusive group of immigrants that entered western North Carolina and eastern Tennessee in the seventeenth and eighteenth centuries, replacing Mississippian communities such as the one located at Hiwassee Island (Lewis and Kneberg 1946:98–99).

In the 1960s, the University of North Carolina at Chapel Hill (UNC) embarked on a long-term research program specifically aimed at constructing a detailed archaeological sequence for the Appalachian Summit region of western North Carolina. Through archaeological surveys, large-scale excavations at selected sites, and artifact analyses, researchers constructed a model of cultural development that countered the migration models proposed by earlier researchers. The UNC model favored the long-term in situ development of the eighteenth-century Cherokee Middle, Valley, and Out towns (represented archaeologically by the Late Qualla phase) from local South Appalachian antecedent cultures whose tenure in the region stretched back at least to the Middle Woodland period (ca. A.D. 200) (Coe 1961; Dickens 1976, 1979; Egloff 1967; Keel 1976).

UNC archaeologists Bennie Keel (1976) and Roy Dickens Jr. (1979) in particular fleshed out a prehistoric trajectory in which the hallmarks of Cherokee culture (i.e., stamped pottery, mound building, and agriculture) first appeared during the Woodland period and continued (if only in vestigial form) until Cherokee removal in 1836. In their model, Woodland period South Appalachian communities evolved to a zenith of sociopolitical complexity during the prehistoric Pisgah phase (ca. A.D. 1000–1550) only to suffer a period of cultural decline and European acculturation during the succeeding Qualla phase (ca. A.D. 1550–1836). Later, Dickens (1986) retreated from a strict in situ model of Cherokee origins. In its place, he offered a multicausal model for Cherokee historical development that combined the notion that Cherokee culture was a distinct adaptive response to the environmental constraints imposed by the South Appalachian region with the notion of cultural transformations brought about by large population movements during the sixteenth century (Dickens 1986:89–90).

In the 1970s, the University of Tennessee conducted a major research program involving archaeology in eastern Tennessee. This program, known as the Tellico Archaeological Project, focused on portions of the lower Little Tennessee valley that would be inundated by the construction of the Tellico Dam. Data recovered by this project led Gerald Schroedl (1986) to construct a different sort of in situ model of Cherokee origins in eastern Tennessee. Although Schroedl (1986:132) viewed eighteenth-century Overhill Cherokee towns as the descendants of earlier sixteenth-century Mississippian chiefdoms, he envisioned a rather different developmental trajectory than the progressive one described by Dickens. Schroedl instead argued that the Overhill Cherokee represented a society that emerged out of the dramatic collapse and reorganization of hierarchically organized chiefdoms during the seventeenth century. This hypothesized regional process has been difficult to verify, however, given a lack of data associated with seventeenth-century Overhill Cherokee occupations (Schroedl 1986; Schroedl, ed. 1986:533).

Research regarding the prehistoric ancestry of Cherokee Lower Towns was furthered by David Hally's (1986a) analysis of pottery from sixteenth- and eighteenth-century contexts in northern Georgia. Using collections recovered from University of Georgia excavations at historically documented eighteenth-century Lower Cherokee towns in the upper Savannah River basin (Kelly and de Baillou 1960; Kelly and Neitzel 1961), Hally (1986a) found a number of similarities in vessel form and surface treatment between sixteenth-century Tugaloo phase assemblages and early eighteenth-century Estatoe phase assemblages. From these similarities, Hally concluded that the pottery associated with historic Cherokee Lower Towns likely developed out of a local ceramic tradition practiced during the late sixteenth century.

Most recently, Christopher Rodning (2002) has offered a reconciliation of the different models of Cherokee ancestry. Rodning's (2004) research at the Coweeta Creek site in southwestern North Carolina is crucial to any discussion of Cherokee origins, as it addresses the seventeenth century, a period for which little is known in eastern Tennessee and northern Georgia. Rodning (2002:157) argues that the emergence of Cherokee identity was a regional phenomenon that largely took place during the late seventeenth and early eighteenth centuries. He states that the manifestation of this shared identity was a complex historical process involving the consequences of long-term developmental trajectories and short-term strategies resulting from European contact. Rodning's model acknowledges that the Cherokee were, at least in part, the descendants of local prehistoric South Appalachian chiefdoms. At the same time, Rodning recognizes that European contact led to dramatic demographic changes and population movements that resulted in a diverse ethnic composition of Cherokee towns. Rodning (2002:159) likens the formation of a shared Cherokee identity to similar processes modeled for the historic Creek by Knight (1994) and for the Choctaw by Galloway (1995).

Research Addressing Cherokee Culture Change

In addition to questions of origins, archaeologists have also tackled problems of change and stability in Cherokee lifeways stemming from European interaction. Presently, there are tantalizingly few securely dated English Contact period Cherokee contexts that appear in publications (e.g., Harmon 1986; Rodning 2004; Schroedl 1994; Shumate et al. 2005; Walker 1995), hence the picture of Cherokee culture change and stability during this period is much less clear than that for the mid-eighteenth century and later.

What we do know about Cherokee culture change during the late seventeenth and early eighteenth centuries is derived from minor occupations at three prominent Overhill Cherokee towns and a Middle Cherokee town, a single Lower Town, and an isolated brief household occupation in southwestern North Carolina. The Tellico Archaeological Project included excavations at historically documented Overhill Cherokee towns in the lower Little Tennessee valley including Citico, Chota-Tanasee, Mialoquo, Tomotley, Toqua, and Tuskegee (Baden 1983; Chapman 1979; Guthe and Bistline 1981; Polhemus 1987; Russ and Chapman 1983; Schroedl, ed. 1986). While some English Contact period contexts were present at Chota-Tanasee, Citico, and Toqua, the vast majority of these data were related to middle and late eighteenth-century Cherokee occupations (Schroedl 2000:215). Another small late seventeenth- and early eighteenth-century occupation including two townhouses was present at the Coweeta Creek site (Rodning 2004). Excavations at the Lower Cherokee town of Chattooga revealed a substantial English Contact period occupation; however, much of that work remains to be published (Howard 1997; Schroedl 1994; Walker 1995). More recently, researchers have reported on a brief middle to late seventeenth-century Cherokee household occupation at the Alarka farmstead site in southwestern North Carolina (Shumate et al. 2005).

While the current body of data regarding late seventeenth- and early eighteenth-century Cherokee communities is less robust than desired, there are nevertheless a few interesting, if preliminary, points that have been made regarding change and stability through the period. First, the architectural forms in these settlements evince little change. Domestic structures consisted of paired winter and summer houses and associated outbuildings (Howard 1997; Schroedl 2000). Winter houses, or *asi*, were substantially built round or octagonal structures averaging 7 m in diameter with central hearths and bench-lined interior walls (Keel 1976:28–34; Schroedl 2000; Schroedl, ed. 1986:267; Shumate et al. 2005). Summer houses were more lightly built rectangular structures averaging 9 by 5.5 m that were erected adjacent to the winter house (Schroedl 2000; Schroedl, ed. 1986:268; Shumate et al. 2005). This type of paired-structure domestic architecture has clear sixteenth-century antecedents across the South Appalachian region (Hally 2002). Major changes in domestic structures did not occur until the late eighteenth century, when interior storage cellars began to appear and single rectangular houses and cabins replaced paired structures as the dominant house form (Riggs 1989; Schroedl 2000:220–223).

The other major structure type in Cherokee communities was the townhouse. Overhill townhouses were large octagonal structures measuring 16 m in diameter with four large support posts, prepared clay hearths, and bench-lined interior walls (Schroedl 2000; Schroedl, ed. 1986:263–266). Adjoining summer townhouses or pavilions were rectangular structures that were similar to domestic summer houses, only larger. The superimposed townhouses at the Coweeta Creek site were not octagonal but instead were square with rounded corners, and they had corner wall-trench entrances (Rodning 2004:365–368). A similar design was identified at Chattooga, where four superimposed square-with-rounded-corner townhouses were found (Howard 1997; Schroedl 1994). The Chattooga townhouses were different from the Coweeta Creek townhouses in that they lacked wall-trench entrances.

While there was geographic variability in the design of these late seventeenth- and early eighteenth-century townhouses, the townhouse sequences at each of these sites demonstrated considerable consistency through time. Throughout the eighteenth century, Overhill townhouses retained the same shape, size, and basic configuration, but the number of internal roof supports increased from four to eight after mid-century (Schroedl, ed. 1986:540). Schroedl (2000:220) suggests that the later form of townhouse likely reflected changes in village demography and the increasingly important role of clans in village life. Particularly, he argues that the new townhouses contained seven partitioned benches, perhaps reflecting the seven matrilineal clans in Cherokee villages. The same trend was evident in the townhouse sequence at Chattooga, although the increase in internal roof supports took place before 1740 (Howard 1997; Schroedl 1994, 2000:214). The early eighteenth-century townhouse at Coweeta Creek was the last of six superimposed structures that were built in the same style over a 200-year period (Rodning 2004:365–368).

The spatial organization of structures within late seventeenth- and early eighteenth-century Cherokee towns appears to have changed considerably from that of earlier sixteenth- and seventeenth-century towns in the region. Earthen mounds were not nearly as common in late seventeenth- and early eighteenth-century Cherokee towns as they were in earlier times, and rarely did these mounds serve as platforms for townhouses (Rodning 2004:68). Public architecture surrounded by open plazas remained a foundational spatial relationship of towns until the nineteenth century; however, the density of settlement amidst this combination changed drastically (see Chapter 5). Whereas sixteenth-century towns like the King site in Georgia and Ledford Island in eastern Tennessee were compact and densely settled, evidence from Chattooga, Chota-Tanasee, and Coweeta Creek suggests that domestic structures were widely spaced within English Contact period Cherokee towns (Rodning 2004:418–419; Schroedl, ed. 1986:539). At the Coweeta Creek site, this switch from intensive to extensive community patterns took place sometime during the late seventeenth century. Rodning (2004:41, 419) suggests depletion of local resources and an increased sense of individualism associated with participation in European trade economies as possible causes for this shift in community patterning.

Existing data suggest that the foodways of seventeenth- and eighteenth-century Cherokee communities remained fairly unchanged from those of the pre-Contact period. Analyses of floral and faunal remains from Coweeta Creek (seventeenth century), Chattooga (early eighteenth century), and Chota-Tanasee (mid-eighteenth century) have demonstrated that pre-Contact food resources, including the corn-beans-squash triumvirate, wild plants, nuts, fish, deer, and bear, dominated the Cherokee diet (Bogan et al. 1986; Schroedl 2000; VanDerwarker and Detwiler 2000, 2002; Walker 1995). A recent study of ceramics from the Coweeta Creek site further demonstrated that the mix of vessel forms in the typical Cherokee domestic pottery assemblage remained consistent from the sixteenth to the eighteenth century; only in the nineteenth century do large amounts of European-made ceramics and metal cooking vessels appear (Riggs and Rodning 2002; Wilson and Rodning 2002).

Contrary to the opinion of Indian agent Thomas Nairne in 1708 (Nairne 1988 [1708]:76), archaeological evidence and ethnohistorical evidence do not support the notion that the Cherokee were materially dependent on European trade goods during the late seventeenth and early eighteenth centuries (see Chapter 2). The assemblages of European-made artifacts recovered from the seventeenth- and early eighteenth-century Cherokee occupations at Coweeta Creek, Chattooga, and Chota-Tanasee were relatively small and included such items as drawn glass beads, kaolin pipe fragments, ornaments and fragments of cut brass, buttons, gun flints, gun parts, iron wedges, iron blades, and bottle glass fragments (Harmon 1986; Newman 1986; Rodning 2004). Only six glass beads and a single iron wedge were recovered from the seventeenth-century Cherokee household occupation at the Alarka farmstead site in southwestern North Carolina (Shumate et al. 2005). But for the absence of perishable goods like cloth and blankets, these assemblages match what would be expected with the early deerskin trade—a time that preceded significant changes in Cherokee material culture associated with the adoption of European technologies (Crane 2004:116–117; Hatley 1995:46–47; Oatis 2004:190–191).

An Alternative Approach to the Archaeology of English Contact Period Cherokee Communities

The various research projects outlined above share common historical and theoretical foundations. They locate Indian communities within a similar landscape—one constructed by early twentieth-century historians and ethnologists like Mooney (1900), Swanton (1998), and Crane (2004). This landscape is set in the perpetual ethnographic present and is inhabited by eternally discrete Indian groups (i.e., tribes or nations) such as "T"he Creek and "T"he Cherokee. In such a landscape, Indian communities become little more than placeholders—basic culture-bearing units whose particular histories are completely interchangeable. This serene and stable landscape constructed by twentieth-century ethnologists and historians must be replaced by the dynamic, chaotic, and inherently unstable landscape that I will describe in Chapter 2. I concur with Rodning (2002:157) that Cherokee ethnogenesis took place largely in response to European colonial pressure during the late seventeenth and early eighteenth centuries. Consequently, I argue that we need to treat the previously independent research problems of Cherokee origins and culture change as parts of the same historical process of identity construction during this tumultuous period. In doing so, I propose a new performative definition of community that takes advantage of archaeology's unique ability to link material culture to the routines of daily life, for these are the foundational behaviors that constituted Cherokee households and communities.

The new tumultuous picture of the southeastern landscape during the seventeenth and early eighteenth centuries necessarily forces us to rethink existing constructs of Cherokee origins (e.g., Dickens 1979; Lewis and Kneberg 1946; Schroedl 1986). Rodning (2002) has pointed out that the process that resulted in the forging of the Cherokee identity likely involved a combination of all three existing models. There was a preceding political collapse and reorganization in the region as argued by Schroedl (1986). There likely was an influx of people from outside of the region after this collapse as postulated by Lewis and Kneberg (1946), and population movement within the region likely occurred as argued by Dickens (1979). With the exception of that of Lewis and Kneberg (1946), however, these models locate the origins of the Cherokee within an extended period of cultural development on the order of centuries. Historic and archaeological evidence suggests that culture change proceeded on the order of decades rather than centuries; therefore, we must place more emphasis on this particular period in our models of the origins of the Cherokee. We also need to localize our models to consider each region within Cherokee territory separately. Part of this includes considering the possibility that the processes that created Overhill Cherokee identity might have been drastically different from those that created, for example, Lower Cherokee identity.

The ethnic composition of native communities must also be reconsidered in light of this dynamic landscape. As mentioned above, there has been a long tradition in American archaeology and ethnology of tying historically documented Indian groups to the landscape through the construction of post hoc in situ histories. Recently, anthropologists and historians have revisited the historic development of groups like the Creek, Choctaw, and Catawba and found that these were not ethnically homogenous tribes or nations but instead were multiethnic confederacies that formed in the seventeenth and early eighteenth centuries in response to the historical forces described in Chapter 2 (i.e., depopulation, slave trade, deerskin trade) (e.g., Galloway 1995; Knight 1994; Merrell 1989a). The term *coalescent societies* is used throughout this study to refer to these ethnically diverse Indian towns (*sensu* Kowalewski 2006). Rodning (2002) recently hinted at the possibility of comparing the formation of the Cherokee to that of these other groups. We know little, however, about the types of ethnic diversity that were present in Cherokee settlements during this period.

Addressing the concept of acculturation, the classic view taken by many researchers of historic Indian groups in the Southeast stressed the increasing rate of adoption of European material culture through time as a reflection of an increasing change to European lifeways (e.g., Brain 1979; Schroedl, ed. 1986). These researchers used the presence and quantity of European artifacts at archaeological sites as proxies to gauge the types of behaviors that were changing. Examples of this include the substitution of items of native construction with European-made items, such as ceramic cooking jars with brass kettles and bows and arrows with guns. While material culture substitutions like these were doubtless an important part of Indian strategies to adapt to the challenges brought about by a growing European colonial presence, simply evoking the process of acculturation to explain why they occurred does not result in an appreciable understanding of the historical process(es) that actually took place.

Worth (2006:204), for example, argues that the acculturation concept treats material culture itself as the primary cause of culture change among Indian and European groups, rather than looking to changes in social, economic, and political structure that may have influenced the change in material culture. He also argues that the concept of acculturation draws attention away from change within Indian groups that may have been completely internal. He asks how acculturation could predict the shift in many native societies from being hierarchical agriculturally based chiefdoms to more egalitarian political groups whose economy was based on trade in deerskins and slaves. Furthermore, Esarey (2007) has shown that the acculturation concept simply does not predict the nature and scale of culture change experienced by seventeenth-century Indian communities in the upper Midwest. In this region, massive social and political disruptions preceded sustained contact with Europeans by several decades. Such a situation is analogous to that experienced by English Contact period Cherokee communities who, unlike neighboring groups in the Southeast, did not experience sustained contact with European traders until the second decade of the eighteenth century.

These critiques challenge us to seek ways to identify changes in English Contact period Cherokee communities other than by counting European artifacts. In this study, I depart from previous historical and archaeological treatments in that I explore change at the Townsend site by emphasizing how the strategic actions of Cherokee households played into larger historical processes of identity construction associated with the tempestuous landscape of the late seventeenth- and early eighteenth-century Southeast. How can this approach be linked to the archaeological record? Answering this question requires two theoretical shifts: (1) the replacement of *community* as a conceptual placeholder with *community* as the outcome of a myriad of performances by constituent members (I focus on households) and (2) the understanding that history was continually being made and remade through the playing out of strategies that had material dimensions and thus had correlates in the archaeological record (I focus on settlement patterns, pottery, architecture, and subterranean pit features).

Past research on southeastern Indian groups like the Cherokee has demonstrated that their communities were not bounded, static locations on the landscape; instead, they were fluid socially constituted collectivities of individuals linked through shared identities (Rodning 2002, 2004:7; Smith 1979; Swanton 1928:242). These communities were created by the shared practices of people who interacted on a daily basis (*sensu* Joyce and Hendon 2000; Norval 1996; Watanabe 1992; Yaeger and Canuto 2000). Through daily interactions, community identities were created, and these community identities, in turn, acted to shape the practices of community members (Anderson 1991). This dialectical process is recognizable in the material traces of daily life at the household level, which represents the most fundamental and pervasive unit of economic and social production (e.g., Blanton

1994; Conkey 1999; Hatch 1995; Hodder and Cessford 2004; Lightfoot et al. 1998; Muller 1997; Pauketat 2000a, 2001; Riggs 1989; Schroedl 1989; Wilk and Netting 1984; Wilk and Rathje 1982). Hence, the strategies enacted by households in Cherokee communities should be visible in the archaeological remnants of daily domestic practice (see Wesson 2008 for a similar study involving Creek households).

The daily practices of English Contact period Cherokee households doubtless operated on discursive and nondiscursive levels, both of which had material dimensions. Discursive practices make obvious statements regarding Cherokee identity. Examples of this type of practice might have included, in part, the choice of community or household location or the architectural design of a house. Nondiscursive practices, on the other hand, involved habitual everyday acts like making a ceramic pot or cooking a meal that, although not necessarily unconscious, were often "taken for granted" (Bourdieu 1977:79; Giddens 1979:24). Recent studies have demonstrated that these tacit practices are indeed fruitful avenues of inquiry for showing how identities were created and passed on generationally (Dobres 1999, 2000; Sinclair 2000; Stark 1998).

In the following chapters, I apply these concepts to a study of the Townsend site (40Bt89–40Bt91), a small English Contact period Cherokee community located in eastern Tennessee. This particular case study will provide a very good example of how the shatter zone (Ethridge 2006) impacted daily life in English Contact period Cherokee communities and, conversely, how the shatter zone was created and perpetuated in the daily practices of Cherokee households. My study is presented in five chapters. Chapter 2 provides a detailed examination of the historical context encompassing the English Contact period. In this chapter, I combine information from published secondary sources as well as primary sources to describe the social, political, and economic landscape inhabited by the Cherokee in the late seventeenth and early eighteenth centuries. The remainder of my study focuses on how the households of the Townsend site community adapted to this newly evolving landscape in three aspects of daily life:

• *Geography.* In Chapter 3, I introduce the case study for my research within a broader discussion of Cherokee geography and settlement patterns. I find that the physiographic setting of the Tuckaleechee Towns, a large and fertile floodplain within a protected mountain cove, would have provided a key advantage to groups who sought a bulwark against the threat of disease and violence. I argue that the location of the Townsend site reflects a strategic settlement pattern response to the shatter zone.

• *Community Identity.* In Chapter 4, I provide a discussion of the household pottery assemblages from the Townsend site. This discussion focuses on characterizing interhousehold ceramic variability as a product of a collection of resident potters practicing distinct regional potting traditions. The high degree of diversity in pottery assemblages, and their discrete distribution among households, leads me to argue that a significant number of individuals in the Townsend community were most likely emigrants from other Cherokee settlements. Together, these households formed a coalescent society—an improvised community that was a strategic response to the turmoil happening around them.

• *Domestic Space and Time.* These related dimensions of daily life are often overlooked in archaeological studies. In Chapter 5, I make a diachronic regional comparison of architectural data sets in order to explore how the spacing and tempo of daily life changed dramatically in Cherokee communities during the English Contact period. I find that the Townsend site, as well as other post-Contact Cherokee communities, lacked the highly structured spatial organization and long-lived residential areas that typified pre-Contact Mississippian communities in the region. From this evidence, I conclude that the chaotic social, political, and economic landscape inhabited by these Cherokee households necessitated a radical, yet strategic shift from practices emphasizing continuity with the past to those aimed at negotiating an uncertain future.

Finally, in Chapter 6, I present a historical narrative of the strategies enacted by Cherokee households in their attempts to adapt to life in the late seventeenth- and early eighteenth-century Southeast.

2

Pox, Empire, Shackles, and Hides

Defining the English Contact Period in the Southeast, 1670–1715

Differences in epistemology and methodology separate the many scholarly disciplines studying the past (e.g., literature, archaeology, history, paleontology); however, all are united by a shared concern with reconstructing the world in which their study objects once existed. Historians have done a great deal of this sort of contextual reconstruction in writing about the Cherokee in the late seventeenth and early eighteenth centuries (e.g., Corkran 1962, 1967; Crane 2004; Gallay 2002; Hatley 1995; Oatis 2004; Reid 1976). In this chapter, I outline the historical context for the English Contact period in the Southeast beginning with the founding of Charles Town (Charleston) in 1670 and ending with the outbreak of the Yamasee War in 1715.

My discussion focuses on the period leading up to the Yamasee War because I believe that the historical processes operating during this period were crucial in setting the stage for the rest of the eighteenth century. I outline three historical forces that I believe were instrumental in forging a landscape of disruption across the Southeast (Figure 2.1). The interplay of these three forces, which included epidemic disease, European colonial competition, and trade in Indian slaves and deerskins, produced massive demographic and sociopolitical turmoil whose effects forever altered the histories of Indian groups and colonists (Bowne 2005; Ethridge 2006; Gallay 2002; Riggs 2010; Wood 1989). The Yamasee War was in many ways the capstone of the English Contact period in that it marked the culmination of disruptions caused by the three historical forces.

Given that the English Contact period was not some monolithic regional phenomenon, I take the approach that each case should ultimately

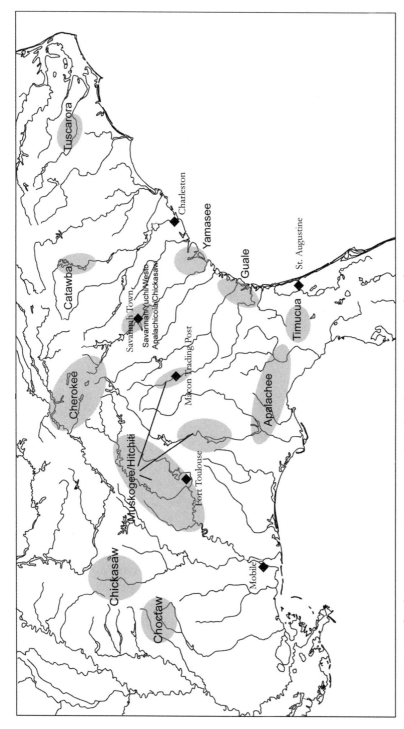

Figure 2.1. Map of Indian groups and European colonial settlements mentioned in the text.

be viewed as representing a complex and highly contingent local history of Indian and European strategic interaction. Consequently, after presenting my historical outline I rely on historical syntheses and primary documents to explore the particular strategies that Cherokee groups appear to have enacted while negotiating this turbulent period.

THE "SHATTERED" PATH TO THE YAMASEE WAR, 1670–1715

Until very recently, the historiography of the period leading up to the Yamasee War had been presented as a singular narrative. Originally put forth in the 1920s by the venerable historian Verner W. Crane (2004) and the equally esteemed anthropologist John R. Swanton (1998), this narrative presented a relatively straightforward picture of the Yamasee War as a "far reaching revolt" of numerous southeastern tribes spurred on by indebtedness to and mistreatment at the hands of Carolinian traders (Crane 2004:162; Swanton 1998:97). This classic explanation has been challenged recently with a series of historical and ethnohistorical works. The authors of these works argue that the established explanation for the Yamasee War is overly simplistic (e.g., Gallay 2002; Martin 1994; Oatis 2004; Ramsey 2001). In the place of a singular process (i.e., *the cause* of the war), these authors characterize the Yamasee War as the outcome of a complex mix of strategies and events that were enacted and experienced differently by the various participants. Instead of lumping all Indian groups into the singular role of reactionaries against the English traders, the authors of these works explore the varied strategies pursued by Indian groups as they interacted with other Indian groups, colonial traders, and colonial governments.

As part of this movement, Robbie Ethridge (2006) has employed the *shatter zone* concept to frame her ethnohistorical reconstruction of the southeastern colonial landscape during the late seventeenth and early eighteenth centuries. This theoretical concept is derived largely from Eric Wolf's (1982) arguments regarding the intense social, political, and economic instability that occurs with the introduction of a capitalistic trading system into "traditional" societies (see also Abler 1992, Ferguson and Whitehead 1992, and Law 1992 for research focusing on the effects of European colonialism on indigenous warfare). One interesting feature of this model is its massive geographical scale. Indeed, the disruptive effects are argued to radiate out from shatter zones like shock waves, covering hundreds of miles (see Esarey 2007 and Jeter 2002 for good examples of the geographic extent of this disruption). Ethridge (2006:208) argues that the whole of the Eastern Woodlands of the United States was a shatter zone in which the raiding activities of a small number of "militaristic slaving societies"—she cites the

Iroquois, Occaneechi, Westo, Chisca, and Chickasaw as examples—set off massive population migrations, amalgamations, and extinctions. In contrast to the traditional view of this period, which has typically sought to find continuity across the protohistoric divide, this new research brings to light a new landscape—one Riggs (2010) rightfully describes as "chaotic."

Through the introduction of the shatter zone concept, Ethridge's (2006) work makes three important points that must be considered when developing a historical context of the English Contact period. First, following the recent critiques of historians mentioned above, any narrative related to this period needs to be regionally nuanced, taking into account the highly variable outcomes of interaction between different colonial and Indian groups. Second, the Indian slave trade should be given a more significant role in our narratives. Third, Ethridge's use of the shatter zone concept compels us to locate historical process physically by mapping it onto the landscape.

I take these points into account in outlining the major historical forces that acted in concert to create the shatter zone(s) across the Southeast during the years leading up to the Yamasee War: (1) the spread of epidemic disease, (2) European colonial competition, and (3) trade in Indian slaves and deerskins.

Pox: Disease and the Shatter Zone

The dramatic effects of European diseases upon native groups across North America are well known (e.g., Dobyns 1983; Milner 1980; Smith 1987; Ward and Davis 1991, 2001). When Europeans came to the New World, they brought infectious diseases like smallpox, measles, yellow fever, typhus, whooping cough, influenza, and plague to New World populations (Kelton 2002:22–23). Because native North American populations had never been exposed to these diseases, outbreaks of sickness grew to epidemics that spread quickly throughout villages and towns, killing many. The period leading up to and including the English Contact period witnessed many of these so-called virgin soil epidemics, the results of which were large-scale regional depopulation; social, economic, and political instability; and mass population movements.

Most researchers would agree that throughout the sixteenth, seventeenth, and eighteenth centuries, European diseases caused dramatic population losses among Indian communities across the Southeast; however, there is debate over the timing and the geographic extent of disease epidemics. Some researchers argue that by the mid-sixteenth century, regionwide "waves" of disease epidemics had already begun to severely affect New World populations (e.g., Dobyns 1983; Romenofsky 1987; Smith 1987). These researchers point to evidence for early regional epidemics across the New World in the sixteenth-century accounts of Spanish explorers. The accounts, which detail travels in South, Central, and North America, describe the effects of great regional pestilences that had preceded the European travelers (Crosby 1972). In the Southeast, researchers like Smith (1987:58) argue that infectious diseases (most likely smallpox) spread inland from coastal contact sites along the conduits of regional trade. While the ethnohistoric evidence Smith (1987:57–60) marshals for the frequency of disease outbreaks in late sixteenth-century Florida is convincing, the accounts mostly speak of localized outbreaks and, as Smith (1987:84) states, the archaeological evidence for regionwide depopulation during this period is rather weak.

Other researchers argue that while disease epidemics did affect southeastern Indian groups during the sixteenth century, these outbreaks were not the massive regionwide epidemics envisioned by Dobyns (1983) and others. These researchers instead argue that epidemics were more likely geographically restricted and that southeastern Indian communities did not experience massive disease-related population losses until they had sustained contact with Europeans in the late seventeenth century (Kelton 2002; Milner 1980; Ward and Davis 1991). Examining the epidemiological nature of smallpox, which he considers the best candidate for a highly infectious and deadly disease, Kelton (2002:25) finds that while deadly and communicable, the disease requires certain conditions in order to spread on a regional scale—namely direct contact. He states that while indirect infection through European trade was possible early on, the relatively low volume of trade in the Southeast during the late sixteenth and early seventeenth centuries would have precluded a regional epidemic. Kelton (2002:31) believes that the conditions necessary for the rapid spread of smallpox emerged only at the end of the seventeenth century, when Charleston traders and Indian groups had established a commercial system of trade in Indian slaves and deerskins that stretched from the Atlantic coast to the Mississippi River. In this high-volume trading system, European traders, Indian hunters, and Indian slaves were all potential disease vectors who circulated widely throughout the Southeast. Kelton believes that this scenario resulted in the first major regionwide smallpox epidemic that wracked many Indian and colonial settlements between 1696 and 1700.

Ward and Davis (1991) tested these two models of disease with archaeological data from sixteenth- and seventeenth-century village sites located in the North Carolina Piedmont. Examining settlement pattern, community pattern, and mortuary data, Ward and Davis (1991:175) found no evidence for massive depopulation during the sixteenth or early seventeenth century. In examining site-level data they did, however, find significant increases in the crude mortality rate and mortuary evidence indicating epidemic episodes (i.e., multiple-individual burials and an overrepresentation of subadults in mortuary populations) in contexts with high frequencies of European trade goods dating to the last quarter of the seventeenth century (Ward and Davis 1991:176–180). In addition, they present period accounts suggesting that disease epidemics struck the Piedmont region in the late seventeenth century. Englishman John Lawson's account of a trip through the region in 1700, for example, describes areas of the North Carolina Piedmont that had suffered massive depopulation (presumably through disease). These areas, which had been occupied by groups intensively trading with Virginians, were contrasted with areas to the south (outside of the bounds of direct trade with Virginians) that were "thickly settled." From this evidence, Ward and Davis conclude that while disease epidemics were a major source of depopulation among North Carolina Piedmont groups, massive outbreaks did not likely occur until after sustained contact with Europeans in the 1670s.

It is a difficult task to quantify the losses endured by Indian groups during the years leading up to the Yamasee War. Fortunately, Peter Wood's (1989) comprehensive compilation of historical population estimates for southeastern Indian groups offers a reliable estimate. Wood examined numerous colonial censuses and historical accounts to arrive at demographic profiles for 10 regions across the Southeast. These profiles included population estimates at 15-year intervals beginning in 1685 and ending in 1790. Wood determined that between the years 1685 and 1715, the Indian population in the Southeast declined from 199,400 to 90,100, a reduction of nearly 55 percent. These are, of course, rough estimates, but the pattern of drastic decline is telling. Slave raiding, warfare, and mass migration account for some of this precipitous decline, but epidemic disease, especially the 1696 smallpox epidemic, was by far the main factor (Wood 1989:90–91).

Empire: European Colonial Competition and the Shatter Zone

The founding of the South Carolina colony at Charles Town in 1670 was not the first attempt by Europe's imperial powers to gain a foothold in the Southeast. The Spanish and French both had established colonies in the Southeast a little less than a century earlier (Crane 2004; DePratter and South 1990). By the middle of the seventeenth century, the Spanish were successfully managing an extensive network of missions throughout northern Florida and along the Georgia coast (Bushnell 1994; McEwan 1993; Worth 1995). Also, as part of the same colonial charter as South Carolina two other settlements had been founded along the present-day North Carolina coast during the 1660s, and by 1670 the Virginia colony had existed for almost three-quarters of a century (Crane 2004:5). Although not the first colony in the region, South Carolina had by far the greatest lasting impact on the Cherokee and other southeastern Indian groups. How did this colony that began as a settlement of 150 or so colonists come to play such a major role in the histories of tens of thousands of Indians and colonial settlers? In answering this question one must look at how South Carolina fit into the larger system of colonial competition involving the imperial ambitions of England, Spain, and France between 1670 and 1715 (Gallay 2002; Oatis 2004).

In 1663, King Charles II of England granted eight "promoter-politicians" a patent for land between 36° and 31° latitude from "sea to sea" (Crane 2004:4). According to the terms of the patent, the colony that was to be settled on this land, called *Carolina,* was to be a proprietary colony. A proprietary colony was different from royal colonies like Virginia in that the Crown granted the proprietors complete control over the laws, distribution of land, and colonial relations with Indians—along with complete financial responsibility for the colony's well-being (Clowse 1971:17–22; Duff 2001; Gallay 2002:43). Proprietary colonies were first and foremost commercial ventures that served to increase the fortunes of proprietors and colonists alike. In the case of the South Carolina colony, this pursuit was attained at first through a brisk Indian trade and, after the turn of the eighteenth century, through the additional development of a substantial plantation economy (Duff 2001).

Because they often lacked the funds to enforce laws and were not directly tied to the Crown, the proprietors and their appointed officials do not appear to have had the same degree of control over colonists as royal colonial officials. Instead, South Carolina was dominated by the mandate of private wealth accumulation (Gallay 2002:63–64). This colonial avarice can be seen best in the promotional pamphlets written by colonists like Thomas Nairne (1989 [1710]) and John Norris (1989 [1712]). While their writings described the geography and environment of the region, the authors spilled much more ink enticing the reader with the profit potentials of a colonist's life spent planting and trading (Greene 1989:9–14). The personal histories of some of the wealthiest men in South Carolina during the period suggest that the most profitable strategy was to combine the Indian trade for slaves and deerskins with planting (Gallay 2002:208–209). This economic structure, in which the profits from trading were used to capitalize the growth of plantations with both funds and slave labor, was in large part responsible for the rise of the Carolina colony within the burgeoning trans-Atlantic economy (Gallay 2002:49; Nash 2001). The highly competitive economic structure also nourished the development of an aggressive risk-taking ethos among South Carolina colonists and officials. During the English Contact period, this ethos appears to have heavily influenced the strategies enacted by South Carolina officials in dealing with their Spanish and French rivals.

The economic and strategic ambitions associated with empire building naturally generated strife among the fragile colonial beachheads of England, Spain, and France (Gallay 2002:2). England and France pursued essentially the same colonial strategy in the Southeast—one founded on the expansionist principles of mercantilism (Gallay 2002:128–132). The Spanish, on the other hand, expressed relatively little interest in extracting economic resources from their southeastern colonies; instead, as early as 1565, King Phillip II of Spain declared that the dual missions of the Spanish colonies in the Southeast were to protect Caribbean shipping lanes and to propagate the Catholic faith among southeastern Indian groups (Oatis 2004:16–17). Regardless of similarities and differences in colonial strategy, it was a fait accompli that the colonies of these three kingdoms would eventually clash in armed encounters in the Southeast. Spain and France were, after all, eternal rivals of England, and violent conflicts among the three colonial superpowers (or more often among their Indian allies) punctuated this period.

Whether it desired the position or not, by virtue of geography South Carolina would be the English colonial vanguard against any southeastern invasion from Spanish or French forces. It did not take long before South Carolina was called to fulfill this role, for immediately after the founding of Charles Town, the Spanish began plotting attacks (Crane 2004:9–10). In August and again in December 1686, the Spanish acted on their plans and mounted attacks that destroyed Stuart Town, a settlement located at Port Royal south of Charleston (Gallay 2002:82–84). This attack so close to their main settlement doubtless gave the South Carolina proprietors good reason to implement a proactive defensive strategy that featured the use of allied Indian groups to create a "buffer zone" that would protect the colony from the Spanish and French and their Indian allies (Gallay 2002:96–97; Oatis 2004:38).

The buffer zone that was to protect South Carolina needed to be strongest to the south in order to check raids by the Spanish and their Indian allies. The Savannah River was the most appropriate location for a border because it was a defensible obstacle as well as a major route of ingress into the interior Southeast (Gallay 2002:71). South Carolina did not have the manpower to construct or man garrisons along the river, thus the colonists had to rely on Indian allies to guard their frontiers. Beginning in the 1680s, colonial officials set about encouraging allied Indian groups to settle along the Savannah River with the construction of a trading post at Savannah Town. By the first decade of the eighteenth century, the trading post had accomplished its mission by attracting numerous allied groups including the Savannah, Yamasee, Apalachicola, Yuchi, and Chickasaw (Gallay 2002:73). The success of the strategy was visible to the colonists as well. In his 1710 promotional pamphlet, for example, Thomas Nairne (1989 [1710]: 53) boasted that "all of the Indians within 700 miles of Charlestown" had been made "their subjects . . . by drawing over to [the colony's] side or destroying" (see also Oatis 2004:83).

It is clear that the South Carolina architects of this strategy never intended for the buffer zone of Indian allies to be a passive deterrent to their European rivals. From their earliest overtures to Indian groups, South Carolina officials intended to create an armed militia of Indians that could be persuaded to promote the colony's interests internally and abroad. Nairne (1989 [1710]:53) wrote of this strategy, saying, "adding to our Strength and Safety . . . [we are] training our Indian Subjects in the Use of Arms, and Knowledge of War, which would be of great Service to us, in case of any invasion from an Enemy." The creation of an allied-Indian buffer zone began in 1673 and 1674 through alliances with the Esaw and Westo, and by 1715 the list of South Carolina's allies grew to include Savannah, Yamasee, Yuchi, Cherokee, Catawba, and Muskogee- and Hitchiti-speaking groups that would later be known as the Creek (Bowne 2005, 2006; Gallay 2002:53–56). The bonds of these alliances were forged through trade in arms, deerskins, and Indian slaves, and South Carolina was able to employ its allies effectively by exploiting both traditional and recently emerged animosities among Indian groups.

Allied Indian groups proved to be invaluable to South Carolina in neutralizing perceived and actual threats to the colony's local interests. The first implementation of this strategy was effected by the Savannah Indians in the 1680s when certain influential South Carolina traders, known as the Goose Creek men, determined that the Westo and Winiah Indians were unstable allies who had become obstacles to their plans (Bowne 2005:100–105). Doubtless spurred on by the promise of income from taking slaves, the Savannah attacked these groups and "cut them off," selling into slavery those who were not killed. Later, between 1707 and 1711, when the Savannah inexplicably began raiding colonial settlements, South Carolina allied with Piedmont Indian groups, many of which later were known as Catawba, to run the Savannah out of the region (Merrell 1989a:52–57).

The Tuscarora War was a similar but more substantial conflict fought in North Carolina in response to Tuscarora raids on European settlers. The war consisted of two military expeditions led by South Carolinians John Barnwell, in 1712, and James Moore Jr., in 1713, along with an assembled force of Yamasee, Apalachee, Cherokee, and Catawba numbering in the hundreds (Oatis 2004:84–91). Although the expeditions were far from exemplars of military planning or execution, they did manage to quell the raids as well as effectively end the Tuscarora's tenure as a viable Indian group in the Southeast (Crane 2004:158–161; Gallay 2002:259–287).

The use of Indian allies was also a potent tool in promoting South Carolina's interests against its European rivals. This strategy was employed on two scales. On one scale were small yet frequent slave raids consisting of parties of 2 to 10 men that were carried out on enemy-allied Indian groups like the Timucua, Apalachee, Guale, Arkansas, and Tunica along South Carolina's borders (Gallay 2002:186, 294–299). The first 15 years of the eighteenth century also witnessed the use of Indian allies on a much larger scale in major colonist-led Indian military forays that cumulatively resulted in the deaths and enslavement of thousands of Indians. These forays included Colonel James Moore's invasions of Spanish Florida as part of Queen Anne's War, first against St. Augustine in 1702 and later against the Apalachee missions in 1704. These operations, which resulted in the destruction of the Spanish-allied Apalachee Indians, included 370 Yamasee Indians and 1,000 Muskogee-speaking Indians, respectively (Crane 2004:79–81; Gallay 2002:136, 145; Oatis 2004:47, 50–51). A third major assault against the Spanish settlement of Pensacola launched in 1707 involved a few hundred Muskogee-speaking warriors (Oatis 2004:70). Against French colonial interests, South Carolina traders and allied Indians conducted an attack on Tomeh and Mobile Indians around the colony of Mobile in 1709 and two attacks on French-allied Choctaw towns in 1705 and 1711 (Crane 2004:85–86; Gallay 2002:288–292). Period accounts reported that the attacks on the Choctaw involved English-allied Chickasaw and Muskogee-speaking forces numbering between 2,000 and 4,000.

A dynamic and unstable cultural landscape was thus created, in part, as an outcome of the economic and diplomatic strategies outlined above. Discussed in greater detail below, the economic structure of the South Carolina colony was the primary engine that drove the colonial side of colonial–Indian relations. Many colonists were engaged in a quest for personal riches, and trade with Indians provided a very high profit margin—especially when the commodities being exchanged were Indian slaves. The creation of South Carolina's buffer zone, which was aimed at protecting the valuable plantations, involved the resettlement of hundreds if not thousands of allied Indians. On the other side of the European imperial rivalry, the brunt of the Carolina-Indian invasions against Spanish and French colonial powers was absorbed by Indian groups. These groups, who suffered the deaths and enslavement of thousands, were also acting as buffers for Spanish and French colonies.

Shackles and Hides: Trade in Indian Slaves and Deerskins and the Shatter Zone

During the English Contact period, the success or failure of any strategy enacted by the European colonial powers was ultimately tied to successful trade with Indian groups. Sustained exchange relations between southeastern Indian groups and Europeans had existed for nearly a century when Charles Town was founded in 1670. Indeed, Smith (1987) and Waselkov (1989) have garnered ethnohistorical and archaeological evidence to demonstrate that small-scale yet substantial trade in deerskins existed between Spanish Florida and interior Indian groups during the late sixteenth and the seventeenth centuries. The founding of English colonies in the Southeast in the 1600s, however, brought about major changes to the existing exchange system. Unlike those of Spanish colonies, the economic structures of South Carolina and Virginia were geared toward generating large profits by producing mass quantities of goods and resources for export. Along with tobacco and rice plantations, Indian trade figured prominently in the economic structure of southeastern English colonies, much more so in South Carolina than in Virginia (Martin 1994:307). It was the scale of Indian trade needed to satisfy the labor and capital demands of both the local plantation economy and the Atlantic trade economy that marked the departure of the English Contact period trading system from the previous Spanish system (Ramsey 2003). The sheer scale of slavery and deer hunting in this system produced profound sociopolitical disruptions that were variably felt by every Indian group across the Southeast.

Until relatively recently, research regarding the trade in Indian slaves had been relegated to isolated anecdotes in the history and archaeology of the seventeenth- and early eighteenth-century Southeast. In classic histories of the colonial Southeast (e.g., Crane 2004; Swanton 1998) one sees references to the taking of slaves in English-Indian raids on Spanish Florida, the Tuscarora War, and Choctaw raids, but the phenomenon of Indian slave raiding is treated from the European perspective as "a less respectable branch of business" that was of "small economic significance" (Crane 2004:109, 112). The attention of a number of scholars, however, has lately been drawn to the phenomenon of the Indian slave trade as a major factor in the histories of the colonies and Indian groups throughout the whole of eastern North America (e.g., Bowne 2005, 2006; Ethridge 2006; Gallay 2002; Ramsey 2001, 2003; Riggs 2010; Usner 1992; Worth 2006).

Historians William Ramsey (2001, 2003) and Alan Gallay (2002) have done much to quantify the scale of Indian slavery by consulting the colonial records of South Carolina. Ramsey (2001:168–169) sketched the historic demography of Indian slavery in South Carolina during the period. Surveying period wills and census records, he found that Indian slaves made up only 6 percent of all slaves during the 1680s and 1690s but that this number rose to 10 percent after Colonel James Moore's raids of 1702 and 1704. By the outbreak of the Yamasee War in 1715, approximately 25 percent of all slaves held by South Carolinians were Indians, a total population of 1,400 individuals. Although the proprietors themselves viewed Indian slavery as illegal, the only restrictions placed on the Indian slave trade by colonial officials were put forth in 1680 and 1691 (Clowse 1971:66–68, 84). These orders, which were nearly impossible to enforce, placed an ambit of 200 miles (in 1680) and 400 miles (in 1691) around Charleston within which no "friendly" Indian could be sold into slavery (Gallay 2002:62; Oatis 2004:38). Ramsey (2003:60) pointed to strong market forces influencing the scale of slave trade during the English Contact period, arguing that the South Carolina economy depended on slave labor not only for working South Carolina's plantations but also for trade to other plantation colonies.

Gallay's research (2002:294–308) furthered the argument that most slaves sold in Charleston markets were later traded to other colonies. He argued that the population estimated by Ramsey was but a small fraction of the total number of slaves taken during this period. Based on transport records following major military campaigns (described above) and trader accounts, Gallay (2002:299) estimated the total number of Indian slaves that were taken between 1670 and 1715 to be between 24,000 and 51,000 individuals. He also contended that most researchers grossly underestimate this figure because of a lack of official documentation in South Carolina records of Indian slave exports to Caribbean and northern mainland colonies (Gallay 2002:299–300). Gallay (2002:301) believed that a large percentage of the trade in Indian slaves was purposefully left undocumented in order to keep secret "an important commodity that was regulated and taxed by the mother country when obtained from Africa." While not able to provide a quantitative analysis, Gallay (2002:301–308) did find ample evidence in early eighteenth-century colonial records and accounts for the presence of southeastern Indian slaves in Caribbean colonies, Massachusetts, Rhode Island, Pennsylvania, New York, and Virginia.

The demand for slave labor in colonial plantation economies was thus a major determinant of the English Contact period trading system, but the supply side of the slavery system must also be considered. Most researchers agree that the taking of slaves by southeastern Indians was a tradition of significant geographic range and time depth (Bowne 2006:128; Dye 2002; Gallay 2002:29; Martin 1994:308). They also agree that during the English Contact period the articulation of capitalistic European colonial economies and Indian slavery altered the nature of this tradition drastically. While the earlier southeastern slave-taking tradition was an occasional practice whose purpose was to augment the ranks of diminished local populations or to attain war captives, slave taking during the English Contact period became what Ethridge (2006:208) calls a profit-driven "commercial" venture. Using the cost-benefit calculus of a typical commercial enterprise, a single slave might fetch as much as 200 skins for an Indian captor. Thus, taking even a few slaves in one raid could provide a hunter with more skins than he could usually procure in an entire hunting season (Ramsey 2001:168).

Historical accounts also indicate that English traders often incited Indian groups to conduct slave raids. Dr. Francis Le Jau, a missionary living near Charleston in the early eighteenth century, expressed a distaste for this practice in his journal, writing, "It is reported that some of our Inhabitants . . . excite them [Indians] to make War amongst themselves to get Slaves which they give for our European goods" and "some white men living or trading among them do foment and increase that Bloody Inclination in order to get slaves" (Le Jau 1956a [1708]:39, 41). Le Jau (1956b [1713]:134) also provided a plausible explanation for Indian participation in slave raiding, stating that in some cases it became the only viable option for paying off astronomical debts accumulated with English traders.

Whether to fulfill desire or necessity, the promise of wealth attained through capturing slaves led to the widespread participation of Indian groups in South Carolina's military campaigns in Queen Anne's War early during the eighteenth century. This new type of commercial slavery led to the meteoric rise (and fall) of so-called militaristic slaving societies whose sole focus (at least from the perspective of colonial records) was "making war" and controlling access to English trade (Bowne 2005, 2006; Ethridge 2006). These heavily armed groups, which included most infamously the Westo but also the Yamasee, Yuchi, Chickasaw, and Savannah (Shawnee), were the major regional players in a European-backed interregional slave-trading system that preyed upon Indian towns stretching from the Carolina and Georgia Piedmont, across the Appalachian Mountains, to the lower Mississippi Valley. Ethridge (2006:211) points out that these groups not only contributed to the formation of the shatter zone in the Southeast but also were themselves likely the product of a ripple effect emanating from the creation of the shatter zone in the Northeast. The ripple effect was manifested in the form of the immigrating Westo, who were originally displaced by Iroquois slave raiding.

The other commodity that circulated within the flourishing colonial trading system was deerskins. Virginians began trading in deerskins with nearby tribes shortly after the colony's founding in 1607, but trade with Indian groups beyond the Carolina Piedmont was at this time insignificant, possibly because the routes to more distant groups were controlled by middlemen like the Occaneechi, Catawba, and Tuscarora (Martin 1994:307; Merrell 1989a:28–29). With the founding of the South Carolina colony, the dynamics of this fledgling trading system changed dramatically. First, the scale of the trade increased greatly with the influx of dozens of new traders, all with aspirations of amassing great riches. Second, the geographic position of Charleston allowed these South Carolina traders to trade directly with interior groups using new routes that did not pass through the territory of the North Carolina Piedmont middlemen. Lastly, the establishment of trade with South Carolina added an alternative source of trade for southeastern Indian groups. This led to competition for the Indian trade not only among the European colonial powers but also (and more intensely) between South Carolina and Virginia (Gallay 2002:53; Martin 1994:309–310).

Scholars have often written of the primary role of the deerskin trade in the early history of the Southeast (e.g., Braund 1993; Crane 2004; Hatley 1995; Martin 1994; Oatis 2004; Waselkov 1998). Indeed, it is well known that the Indian trade dominated South Carolina's economy during the English Contact period (Crane 2004:110; Gallay 2002:44). For many colonists in Virginia and South Carolina, entry into the Indian trade during this period was barred by substantial financial barriers. Extensive inputs of money were required to pay for goods, labor, and transportation, as well as to extend lines of credit (Martin 1994:307). To those who could afford it, the payoffs were obviously worth the investment as the scale of this trade was fitting for an international commercial venture. The annual number of deerskins exported to England averaged 54,000 between 1699 and 1715 but fluctuated from year to year. Major events like the 1704 raids on Spanish Florida, the Tuscarora War in 1711, and the Yamasee War in 1715 had demonstrable effects on the trade (Crane 2004:111–112) (Figure 2.2).

The deerskin trade, while a substantial economic force, was never purely an economic venture. For Indian groups as well as colonial officials, trade was inherently linked to diplomacy and treated as "bonds of peace" (Martin 1994:308; Oatis 2004:53–55; Ramsey 2003:46). As a valuable diplomatic tool during this period of intense colonial competition, the deerskin trade became something to be guarded by colonial governments and used as leverage by Indian groups. From 1670 until 1707, there was little attempt by the South Carolina proprietors to control the deerskin trade. Growing reports of abuses by traders finally pressured officials to pass the 1707 "Act for

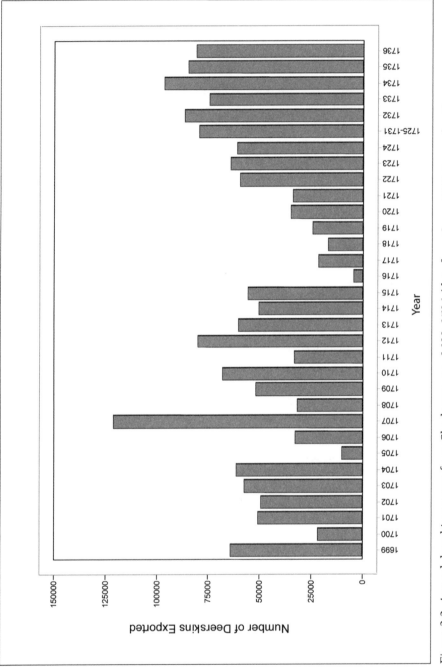

Figure 2.2. Annual deerskin exports from Charleston, A.D. 1699–1736 (data from Crane 2004:Appendix A).

Regulating Indian Trade and Making it Safe to the Publick." This act sought to provide oversight to the trade, to enforce restrictions against selling liquor and free Indians as slaves, and to offer resolution to claims of Indian abuse (Oatis 2004:54). The passage of this act led to the mandatory licensing of all traders and the establishment of the Commissioners of the Indian Trade. A major boon to diplomacy with Indian allies (and colonial intelligence) was the appointment of an Indian agent whose position required him to spend 10 months of the year traveling among major Indian towns (Moore 1988:12). This act and the commission resolved a number of disputes and punished a number of recalcitrant traders, but ultimately these regulatory attempts failed to prevent the coming Yamasee War in 1715.

Competition among colonial powers for trade with various Indian groups was a constant feature of the period, and it is perhaps surprising that the most intense competition occurred not between the three European powers but between two English colonies—South Carolina and Virginia. The French Louisiana colony had sustained trading relations with lower Mississippi Valley groups since the late seventeenth century, and a few *coureurs de bois* had been known to carry on trade with groups as far into the interior Southeast as the upper Tennessee River valley (Crane 1916, 2004:41–43). Lack of substantial colonial backing and the loss of frontier influence after Chickasaw-Muskogean raids during Queen Anne's War (1709–1711), however, prevented the French from making serious advances into the southeastern deerskin trade until after the Yamasee War (Gallay 2002:132–135; Oatis 2004:70–71). The Spanish were even less of a regional competitor for trade during the period. While there was some trade carried on with Muskogean groups in the lower Chattahoochee Valley and with the Yamasee on the South Carolina border, Spanish colonial interests in the Southeast were not focused on expanding trade. Furthermore, the raids carried out by South Carolina and allied Indians effectively ended the expansion of Spanish colonial interests in the Southeast during the first decade of the eighteenth century (Bushnell 1994:161–189; Crane 2004:80–81; Oatis 2004:70–71).

The largest source of competition for the deerskin trade emerged between the English colonies of South Carolina and Virginia. Virginia had the earlier presence in the Southeast, and the accounts of some traders, most notably James Needham and Gabriel Arthur, suggest that by the 1670s Virginia traders had reached Indian groups as distant as the Savannah River and the Gulf of Mexico (Briceland 1987; Bushnell 1907; Franklin 1932; Rountree 2002; Williams 1928). The South Carolinians, however, had the benefit of a more strategic geographic position from which to conduct trade, what appears to be an advantage in numbers of traders, and a zealous (borderline fanatical) approach to competition. The rivalry between the two colonies began almost immediately, with South Carolina wresting trade with the Westo from the Virginians in the 1670s (Gallay 2002:55; Oatis 2004:75). Because of its location, South Carolina appears to have easily bested the Virginians in the deerskin trade with Muskogee-speaking groups and the Chickasaw to the west. The battle over the deerskin trade in the Piedmont and Appalachian Mountains, however, was much less clear-cut. In these regions, it appears that the Virginians were able to maintain a presence by taking advantage of their long-held ties to local communities and by selling their goods at cheaper prices (Merrell 1989a:55).

What effects did the deerskin trade have on southeastern Indian communities? The effects were obviously variable from community to community, but a few general issues were likely widespread. First, as discussed above, the rather inelastic European demand for deerskins and resulting competition between colonies gave certain Indian communities bargaining leverage in dealing with the colonies (Merrell 1989b). This opportunity was certainly exploited by Piedmont Indians, and later with the reemergence of French colonial trade after the Yamasee War, Creek and Cherokee towns did the same (Merrell 1989b; Oatis 2004:215; Waselkov 1993, 1994).

Another important effect of the deerskin trade was the presence in local Indian communities of European traders, many of whom took up full-time residence. Through marriage or less formal arrangements, these traders often became vital members of the local community (Barker 1993, 2001; Hatley 1995:42–51). They acted as indispensable diplomatic envoys who channeled negotiations and intelligence between the Indian towns and colonial officials. The daily presence of the traders in the communities, as well as the offspring of their relationships with local women, also forced the negotiation of cultural differences between Europeans and Indians. As is evident in colonial records, unfortunately these "negotiations" sometimes erupted in violence (Perdue 1998; Ramsey 2003). As Indian groups became more involved in the trade, these resident traders also began to extend lines of credit. While this practice was often necessary given the seasonal nature of deer hunting, in more than a few cases the European traders employed predatory credit schemes that resulted in Indians amassing exorbitant debts. The most extreme example of this situation was the Yamasee, who by 1711 had accumulated a debt of 100,000 skins—roughly twice the annual average of all deerskin exports from South Carolina (Haan 1981:343).

There are also indications that participation in the deerskin trade dramatically altered the histories of particular Indian communities. The historic documents provide numerous examples of communities choosing to move to be closer to European trading posts. These examples include, most notably, the move of Muskogee-speaking groups from the lower Chattahoochee River valley to central Georgia in the 1680s, as well as those of smaller groups of Yamasee, Savannah, Yuchi, and Apalachee to the Savannah River during the early eighteenth century (Gallay 2002:71–73; Waselkov 1994). Of course, there were likely other factors influencing the decision to move, such as harassment by the Spanish or raids by hostile Indian groups; nevertheless, the decision of where to move appears to have been a strategic one made by community members.

On the community level, archaeological excavations at the Muskogean town of Fusihatchee in central Alabama demonstrated that the community ceased to construct domestic "winter" houses around the turn of the eighteenth century. Waselkov (1990:40–41) argued that the winter house may have dropped out of use at this community as hunters and their families spent more time away from their town engaged in extended deer-hunting expeditions for the colonial trade. This interpretation is supported by a concomitant and dramatic increase in the use of long-term subterranean storage in the community after 1700 (Waselkov 1990; Wesson 1999). Together, these patterns suggest that dramatic changes to domestic and community life were occurring as a result of the transformation from a local subsistence economy to one focused on hunting for commercial profits.

The related trade systems involving slaves and deerskins were crucial components in creating across the Southeast the unstable landscape typical of a shatter zone. Slave raiding had a particularly catastrophic effect, resulting in the death or imprisonment of potentially tens of thousands of Indians. The practice also caused massive population movements of groups, motivated by the pursuit of slaves or the threat of enslavement (Smith 1987, 2002). The burgeoning trade in deerskins also resulted in significant changes to Indian communities on the regional and local levels. The dynamic nature of the landscape between 1670 and 1715 was fed by numerous Indian towns that left their traditional territories in order to be closer to European trading posts. Tension was also building within Indian communities as the growing participation in a commercial economy forced the reorganization of domestic life, as resident European traders clashed with local communities, and as families faced mounting debt.

The Yamasee War

On Good Friday, April 15, 1715, the chaos of the shatter zone finally ruptured through the protective buffer surrounding South Carolina and invaded the lives of European colonists. The Yamasee War began that day when a number of South Carolinian trade officials were murdered in the Yamasee town of Pocotaligo. The murders took South Carolinians completely by surprise, as the Yamasee were thought to be one of the colony's closest allies. Indeed, the murdered Englishmen had only been sent to Pocotaligo in order to arrange talks with another Indian group, the Ochese Muskogeans, who were rumored to be planning attacks against South Carolina traders and settlers (Crane 2004:168–169; Oatis 2004:126–127). These initial murders were quickly followed by major Yamasee attacks on plantations around Port Royal, south of Charleston. In these attacks, the Yamasee managed to kill over a hundred colonists and set the rest of the settlement's population to flight (Pennington 1931:253). In the following weeks, news began to filter into Charleston that most of the English traders in the towns of the Tallapoosa, Abiehka, Alabama, Ochese, Coweta, Choctaw, Chickasaw, Catawba, and Cherokee had either been killed or chased off (Oatis 2004:128–132). Adding to the fears of a pan-Indian assault, news emerged that the Catawba and a small group of Cherokee had made raids on plantations north of Charleston and even managed to capture a South Carolina militia garrison (Crane 2004:171–172). Facing this apparent "invasion," colonists across South Carolina fled to Charleston, where the effects of overcrowding, fear, and tension, exacerbated by the summer heat, took their toll on the physical and mental health of many residents (Oatis 2004:140).

Traditionally, historians have written about the Yamasee War as a united Indian revolt against the abuses of English traders, but recent attention has turned to exploring the different motivations and strategies of the Indian groups who participated in the attacks (e.g., Gallay 2002; Merrell 1989a; Oatis 2004; Ramsey 2003). To various extents, these authors agree that while some of the Indian participants were in collusion, the Yamasee War was not a pan-Indian conspiracy carried out with the aid of a master plan (Oatis 2004:123). Instead, they hold that each group acted according to its own strategy and toward its own diplomatic goals. Abuse by traders, mounting debts, and the fear of enslavement were important factors in some groups' decisions to join the war against South Carolina, but these three causes were far from universal. These causes apply most to the Yamasee, but even their decision to attack South Carolina settlements was also likely influenced by the encroachment of Europeans on their treaty-protected lands as well as a breakdown in diplomacy with colonial officials (Gallay 2002:330–331; Haan 1981; Ramsey 2003:46). For Muskogean, Cherokee, Chickasaw, and Choctaw groups, there was no possibility of English settler encroachment during this period, and these groups were far too strong to fear an immediate invasion by English forces.

With this in mind, Gallay (2002:335) interprets the killing of English traders in these groups' towns as a diplomatic message sent to the Carolina officials—the gist of the message being "English promises for reform were no longer acceptable. Alliance was no longer appropriate or possible . . . [The Indians were] announcing to the English the need to negotiate a new relationship." Furthermore, Ramsey (2003:73) argues that the search for general explanations for the cause of the Yamasee War is ultimately fruitless because each Indian group "faced a complex set of local considerations that defy generalization. Common elements shaped their decisions . . . But the nature and value of those elements differed from region to region, and among them stretched a 'thousand threads' that wove them into the local reality."

CHEROKEE STRATEGIES FOR NAVIGATING THE SHATTER ZONE, 1670–1715

What were the highly varied strategies enacted by different Indian groups trying to adapt to a rapidly evolving dialectic with the European colonial powers? Space does not permit an in-depth enumeration or comparison of the various strategies and combinations of strategies that were enacted by all southeastern Indian groups during the English Contact period, but even a cursory examination of current literature reveals that strategies varied from group to group and that the strategies practiced by a particular group changed through time. Groups like the Westo and the Savannah, for instance, chose to move near English trading posts on the Savannah River and to engage heavily in the Indian slave trade (Bowne 2005, 2006; Ethridge 2006). Other groups, like the Kaskinampo and Yuchi, engaged in slavery but largely remained aloof, moving about the periphery of the region in small groups and settling with other small groups for relatively brief periods (Bauxar 1957a, 1957b; Riggs 2010; Swanton 1930). The Creek, Choctaw, and Catawba of the early eighteenth century were large, sedentary, multiethnic confederacies that formed around the nuclei of established Indian towns through the adoption of refugee groups (e.g., Galloway 1995; Knight 1994; Kowalewski 2006; Merrell 1989a). This "strategy of coalescence," as Kowalewski (2006) calls it, appears to have been a very common response to the disruptions of the shatter zone across the seventeenth- and eighteenth-century Southeast (e.g., Davis 2002; Drooker 2002; Hudson 2002; Perttula 2002; Rodning 2002). What were the strategies enacted by Cherokee groups during the English Contact period? My examination of historical syntheses and documents suggests that Cherokee groups practiced yet another strategy—that of isolationism.

Cherokee Isolationism, 1670–1715: "A people little conversant with white men"

When writing the history of the late seventeenth- and early eighteenth-century Southeast, scholars often emphasize the trajectory by which the Cherokee were transformed from "an ambiguous presence" in the mountains to a major focus of colonial trade and diplomacy (Hatley 1995:27). This interpretation is well justified given the relative paucity of extant historical evidence referring to the Cherokee as opposed to other southeastern Indian groups. The few known European maps that date to this period suggest an extremely low level of familiarity with the Cherokee until after the Yamasee War. Furthermore, historic accounts suggest that Cherokee participation in the burgeoning deerskin and Indian slave trade was, for the most part, negligible until after the first decade of the eighteenth century (Crane 2004:41; Hatley 1995:32–33). When compared with other large southeastern Indian groups (e.g., Creek, Chickasaw, Choctaw), all of which were well known to Europeans by the dawn of the eighteenth century, the relative invisibility of the Cherokee becomes intriguing. I suggest that it is possible, and perhaps even likely, that the relative lack of Cherokee involvement in colonial affairs was a measured strategy for surviving in the shatter zone. This strategy was followed by most Cherokee groups until it could no longer be maintained at the beginning of the Yamasee War. In judging the plausibility of this argument, one must consider the fates of groups like the Westo, Savannah, and Yamasee, all of which suffered terrible consequences after developing relationships with South Carolina.

Late seventeenth- and early eighteenth-century maps of the interior Southeast were based on the descriptions of explorers and represented translations of the most current state of knowledge regarding physical and cultural geography (Cumming 1998:20–27; Galloway 1995:205–209). Maps can thus offer a general picture of the degree of knowledge Europeans had of the Cherokee during the English Contact period. The two earliest maps referencing the Cherokee were made in 1682 and 1701 by French cartographers (Swanton 1930). According to Swanton (1930:407–408), the earlier anonymously authored map was based on the descriptions of La Salle and depicted the Tennessee River along with three towns named Tehalaka (i.e., Tchalaka = Cherokee), Cattougai (i.e., Katowagi = Shawnee word for "Cherokee" or Kituwa), and Taligui (i.e., Tellico), all of which Swanton believed were Cherokee towns. If these towns were in fact Cherokee settlements, they were likely located along the Little Tennessee or Hiwassee rivers. Given the inaccuracies of the map, however, the association of these place names with any historically documented towns cannot be accurately determined. The latter map, produced in 1701 by French cartographer Guillaume De l'Isle, was drawn using details provided by a group of *coureurs de bois* who managed to travel to Charleston from the Ohio River valley just prior to 1700 (Crane 1916; Swanton 1930). This map depicts a number of clusters of unnamed villages grouped under the heading "Nation de Tarachis." As with the earlier map, these settlements were also probably located along the Little Tennessee or Hiwassee rivers.

Three English maps dating to this period that show Cherokee settlements are equally vague. Thomas Nairne drafted a map of the Southeast based on his 1708 diplomatic voyage from Charleston to the Mississippi River (Cumming 1998:Plate 45). The original map was lost, but a reproduction was used as an inset in the Edward Crisp map, drawn in 1711. The map depicts a single large cluster of "Cherecie" settlements among the Appalachian Mountains along with a population estimate of 3,000 men. Trader Pryce Hughes also produced a map of his voyage to the Mississippi River around 1713. The original map was lost; however, a copied version dated to 1720 survives (Cumming 1998:23). Like the Nairne map, this work depicts Cherokee settlements with a single caption, "The Cherokees. A great Nation inhabiting within & both sides of the Mountains consisting of 65 Towns." The other English map is an anonymous, undated map that Riggs (2010) argues was drafted two to three years before the Yamasee War (ca. 1712–1713). This map is similar to the De l'Isle map in that it features clusters of settlements simply titled "Charakeys," but it is a more accurate depiction of the distribution of the Upper, Middle, and Lower settlements in their respective river valleys (Cumming 1998:Plate 46A). Taken together, these maps portray the poor but growing state of knowledge of the Cherokee in the late seventeenth and early eighteenth centuries. Individual town names were not known, or at least were not printed, and the locations of settlements were poorly extrapolated from explorer and trader accounts. When viewed as a chronological series, however, the maps suggest that Europeans were coming to understand that the Cherokee represented a formidable population.

When compared with that of other southeastern Indian groups like the Creek, Chickasaw, and Yamasee, Cherokee participation in the deerskin trade during the early English Contact period was a small-scale affair. Cherokee communities were not, however, strangers to European trade. On the contrary, the evidence suggests that by 1670 an unbroken, albeit weak, chain of trade with Europeans had existed for over a century. Links to the Spanish extend back to the late sixteenth and seventeenth centuries in the form of iron tools, brass ornaments, and glass beads that have been recovered from numerous archaeological sites in eastern Tennessee and western North Carolina (Skowronek 1991; Smith 1987; Waselkov 1989). Historical and archaeological evidence suggests that some Cherokee communities were trading with Virginians, at least indirectly, during the last half of the seventeenth century (Briceland 1987; Franklin 1932; Smith 1987). South Carolinians appear to have opened trade with the Cherokee by 1690 (Rothrock 1929). Finally, as indicated by the De l'Isle map, French *coureurs de bois* appear to have established contact with Cherokee communities by 1700 (Crane 1916, 2004:43).

Aside from the accounts detailing these initial contacts, an overall lack of written records suggests that Cherokee settlements were largely forsaken by European traders during this period. The most popular explanation offered by historians for the lack of involvement in the trade is that direct contact with the Cherokee was limited by middlemen or so-called broker tribes. In this gateway model, rather than moving directly to Cherokee towns, most goods were funneled through Piedmont middlemen like the Occaneechi, Catawba, Westo, and Savannah, groups that controlled access to the trading paths from Virginia and South Carolina (Crane 2004:40; Franklin 1932:17–18; Hatley 1995:32–33; Merrell 1989a).

There are two reasons this explanation is not satisfactory. First, it would only apply to the last decades of the seventeenth century, as the military power of many of the Piedmont groups was severely diminished in wars with Virginia and South Carolina in the 1670s and 1680s (Bowne 2005; Davis 2002; Gallay 2002). In fact, of all of the groups, only the Catawba survived as a viable military force into the eighteenth century. Second, the gateway explanation does not account for the meteoric rise of South Carolina trade with the Creek, Chickasaw, and Choctaw, groups with whom contact was established at the same time as the Cherokee. Trade to these groups followed the same route as trade to the Cherokee and would have passed through the same Savannah River valley towns of the Piedmont broker tribes, yet there is ample evidence that English traders were engaged in brisk direct trade with these groups by the turn of the eighteenth century (Crane 1916:17, 2004:25–26; Gallay 2002:161).

The gateway explanation suffers from the assumption that all Indian groups were actively seeking trade with Europeans. Proponents of the model accept as a starting point a great Cherokee demand for European goods, and then they look for outside factors that must have limited Cherokee participation. It would doubtless be fruitful to include questions of Cherokee demand in our explanations rather than limiting the search solely to external explanations. Indeed, the few surviving late seventeenth- and early eighteenth-century accounts of Cherokee traders seem to indicate that the Cherokee were not exactly clambering to get ahold of direct English trade.

Numerous accounts spanning from 1690 to 1713 agree that English traders were quite contemptuous of the general lack of interest in trade shown by the Cherokee. James Moore, eventual governor of South Carolina and leader of the raids on Spanish Florida during Queen Anne's War, is generally credited with opening trade with the Cherokee in a trip to the Appalachian Mountains in 1690. A brief passage from his account, quoted by Crane (2004:40–41), presages the frustrations that would be felt by traders for the next three decades. Crane wrote that Moore "was prevented from penetrating 'to the place which I had gon to see' by 'a difference about Trade . . . between those Indians and me.'" The "difference about Trade" included the killing and enslavement of several Cherokee by Moore's party (Oatis 2004:35–36). The unfortunate outcome of this encounter caused the colonial assembly to pass a ban on private trading west of the Savannah River Indian towns in 1691 (Crane 1916:8n, 2004:41).

In a contemporary account penned in 1690, trader John Stewart commented on Moore's trip as well as the prospects of trade with other southeastern Indian groups:

> C. Moor [James Moore] got not much by his Cherakee voyage, all charges and prime cost deducted he is accoasting our Governor to have a license from him as general to go a 2^d voyage to the Tireaglis [Yuchi?] a people west of the Cherokees he tels me he wes 4 dayes J^{uny} west of the Mountaines in pleasant Valeys until a branch of Canada stop't his further advance. George Smith has returned with 2800 skins and fur from the Cowetas and he wes within 3 or 4 days Jurnay of the bay of Apalatier and hes brought the Coweta and Cusheda K^s here with him, Who have now return'd loaded with presents: they have, being 2500 fighting men, deserted the Spanish protection and com'd and setl'd 10 days Jurnay nearer to us to Injoy the English frier protection [Stewart 1931 (1690):29–30].

This account provides a valuable snapshot of the major events affecting South Carolina's Indian trade at the end of the seventeenth century. Stewart's writings were replete with discussions of "get rich quick" schemes and investment-return calculus indicating that if he lived today he would likely be a venture capitalist. Indeed, Stewart appears to have had a short but successful career as a resident trader with the Kasita, Tallapoosa, and Chickasaw (Gallay 2002:156–164). His negative impression of the Cherokee trade was thus likely shared by other profit-driven traders. Further suggesting a quick dismissal of the Cherokee, Stewart noted that upon his return from the Cherokee voyage, James Moore petitioned the governor not for permission to return to the Cherokee but instead for permission to trade with the "Tireaglis," possibly a group of Yuchi who were settled in the Middle Tennessee River valley of northern Alabama (Bauxar 1957a, 1957b; Fleming 1976; Riggs 2010; Swanton 1930). Stewart's letter indicates that he was more interested in discussing the recent opening of direct trade with the towns of Coweta and Kasita and their removal from the lower Chattahoochee Valley to the Macon Plateau (see also Corkran 1967:50–51). Two important implications can be drawn from Stewart's account. First, early in South Carolina's trade the Cherokee were dismissed by at least some English traders in favor of Muskogee-speaking groups to the west. Second, the traders' attitudes toward different Indian groups were based on their perception of relative profitability. Hence, the proactive strategies of some groups, like the Coweta and Kasita towns who engaged the traders by moving closer to Charleston, certainly made them more attractive trading partners than groups like the Cherokee who did not actively pursue trade.

A 1708 census compiled by Nathaniel Johnson, governor of South Carolina, and his council mimicked the English perception that the Cherokee were apathetic toward trade. The census offered population estimates and brief descriptions of "The Indians under the protection of this Government," including the Yamasee, Apalachee, Savannah, Ochese, Tallapoosa, Chickasaw, Cherokee, and Northward Indians (Piedmont groups like the Catawba). The entry regarding the Cherokee stated: "The Chereky Indians live about two hundred & fifty miles northwest from our settlement [Charleston] on a Ridge of Mountains they are a numerous people but very Lazy they are settled in sixty towns & are at least five thousand men the trade we have with them is Inconsiderable they being but ordinary Hunters & less Warriors" (Johnson et al. 1708:209). This brief description demonstrates that South Carolina's knowledge of the Cherokee was improving by the close of the first decade of the eighteenth century. It provided relatively accurate estimates of the Cherokee population and the total number of towns they had settled at the time, although there was no mention of any town names. The passage also demonstrates that at the same time South Carolinians' knowledge of Cherokee demography was improving, their opinion of the Cherokee as traders was not. The Cherokee were described as "Lazy" and the trade with them "Inconsiderable" (capitalization in the original document).

A letter from English trader Pryce Hughes written in 1713 highlighted the continued English ignorance of the Cherokee even into the second decade of the eighteenth century. The letter also provided considerable detail regarding cultural practices, warning that "The many accounts we've had of the American Indians are for the most part fabulous & imperfect" (Hughes 1713).

> When I was amongst the Cherekees (as a people little conversant with whitemen) they enquired very closely of the nature of our Affairs in England; to be sure I was not wanting to magnifye its Interest. amongst other things telling them how we were governd by a Woman and that greater successes for the most part attended that sex than the other. they desired me to send that good Woman (for they styld her) a present from them viz a large carpet made of mulberry bark for herself to sit on and twelve small ones for her Counsellours. The choicest of their women went forthwith to work: but at my return they were not all finisht; so that I must defer sending them till a further opportunity. The map [the original has been lost] shews your Grace where this nation is situated; Tis the only one that possesses the Apalachee mountains & is the most numerous & most submissive of all Indians belonging to her Majesty. They live a great way off from any white Settlement & so are but little known to us. Of the many nations I've seen these keep up their old customs in their greatest purity. They acknowledge several Deities inferior to that great one above: whom they sacrifice to looking up at the sun. They observe the feast of first fruits & have cities of refuge for the man-slayer to fly to as the Orientals had. Their Priests are for the most part Diviners & Wizards, use fastings & purifications in their religious cere-monyes, & are consulted by the people upon all urgent emergencyes about the success therof, wch they have often times most unaccountably predicted. The younger people are debaucht beyond all belief, which lessens their number daily & will in a little time I fear annihilate their nation. God knows the Infidelity they labour under is little known & were it I believe would be as little regarded. The People however appear very tractable & pliant in the many conferences I had wth their Senators about their conversion [Hughes 1713].

Twice in the letter, Hughes referred to the cultural isolation of the Cherokee from the English. He stated that they are "as a people little conversant with whitemen" and that "They live a great way off from any white Settlement & so are but little known to us." Referring to the fact that Cherokee culture had not yet been significantly altered by contact with Europeans, he stated, "Of the many nations I've seen [which included all of the major southeast-

ern Indian groups] these keep up their old customs in their greatest purity."
Rather than being contemptuous toward the Cherokee, the tone of Hughes's
letter was much more complimentary, even bordering on romantic.

This group of English accounts thus points to a dearth of direct trade
with the Cherokee well into the second decade of the eighteenth century.
What is more, these accounts represent the best source of information regarding the nature of Cherokee trade between 1670 and 1715, for the trade
is rarely discussed in other contemporary colonial records. Licensing records indicate that the first resident traders to the Cherokee were Eleazar
Wiggan in 1711 and Robert Bunning in 1714 (Rothrock 1929:6). The *Journals of the Commissioners of the Indian Trade* (McDowell 1992), which recorded the meeting minutes and correspondence of South Carolina's trade
commission from 1710 to 1718, mentioned the Cherokee only eight times
between September 20, 1710, and April 12, 1715, and half of these were in
reference to a single incident (see discussion of the Chestowee raid below).
The first mention of the Cherokee appeared in the instructions given by the
commission to Indian agent John Wright in 1712. Wright was told "to goe
to the Cherikee Nations and settle all there Grievances and reconcile them
and the Traders" (McDowell 1992:32). Given that the instructions used the
plural forms "Nations" and "traders," it is reasonable to assume that trade
at this time included a number of towns and numerous individuals, but
no specifics were indicated. The only other significant entry regarding the
Cherokee trade before 1715 involved the commission's suspicion that some
recently captured French traders "might have a design to tamper with the
Charikee" (McDowell 1992:45).

Cherokee involvement in the Indian slave trade was minimal when compared with that of groups like the Westo, Savannah, Yamasee, Tallapoosa,
and Chickasaw. In fact, it appears that before 1700 the Cherokee were typically the victims rather than the purveyors of slavery. Between 1700 and
1715 the cases linking Cherokee groups to the slave trade remained few;
however, in these cases, including the infamous Chestowee raid of 1713, it
was the Cherokee who were named as the perpetrators. The first time the
Cherokee Indians appeared in historical records was in a letter recording
trader Henry Woodward's visit to a Westo town in 1674. In this letter, the
"Chorakae" were simply mentioned as enemies of the Westo (Woodward
1911 [1674]:133). Given the Westo's penchant for slave raiding, it is likely
that many Cherokee "enemies" were being taken as slaves in the 1680s
(Hatley 1995:33). By the end of the 1680s, South Carolina colonial documents began to record slave raids against the Cherokee by the Savannah
(Crane 1916:10n, 2004:40; Gallay 2002:94). The toll taken by the Savannah
raids cannot be known, but it must have been quite severe, as the Chero-

kee petitioned the South Carolina government for an intercession in 1691 (Hatley 1995:33).

The Cherokee also had to fear slave raids by Iroquois groups who swept down among their northern towns. In a 1708 letter, England's Earl of Spencer, Thomas Nairne (1988 [1708]:76), briefly mentioned the Cherokee as a potentially valuable ally to South Carolina against the French, noting, "they are now our only defence on the Back parts [the northwestern border of South Carolina] But are themselves miserably harrassed by the Iroquois." Writing a century later, Major John Norton (1970 [1816]:262) recalled that Iroquois warriors began frequently raiding Cherokee and Catawba settlements around 1710.

Historic records contain very few instances of Cherokee slave raids during the English Contact period. For example, during Queen Anne's War there is no mention of any Cherokee taking part in the raids against Spanish-allied or French-allied Indians. In 1705, some Cherokee counseled South Carolina Governor Nathaniel Johnson to curtail the slave trade, imploring him to "trade for skins and furs" rather than "trade of Indians or slave making" (quoted in Martin 1994:313). This warning may have influenced the governor, who said of the Cherokee in the 1708 census, "Trade we have with them is Inconsiderable they being but ordinary Hunters & less Warriors" (Johnson et al. 1708:209). Based on the disparaging judgment of the Cherokee as "Warriors," I believe that the "trade" the governor was referencing was slave trading. This argument is supported by the census's descriptions of the main players in the slave trade (e.g., the Yamasee, Tallapoosa, Alabama, Chickasaw, and Ochese) as "Great Warriors." Furthermore, speaking of the Chickasaw, the census said, "we have but few skins or furs . . . they living so distant . . . [instead we have] . . . Slaves wch we have in Exchange for our Goods with these people taken from severall nations of Indians that live beyond them" (Johnson et al. 1708:209).

If avoiding the slave trade was an intentional strategy, it was one that was not followed by all Cherokee groups, for after 1700 there is evidence that some Cherokee were involved in incidents of slave raiding. As many as 300 Cherokee joined the large Indian contingent that fought during the Tuscarora War in 1713 (Gallay 2002:283; Oatis 2004:89). There is no specific reference of any Cherokee taking slaves in the assaults, but the records are clear that hundreds of Tuscarora were taken as slaves. Three other instances of Cherokee slave raiding were mentioned in colonial documents related to this period. These raids were conducted by much smaller groups than those that participated in the Tuscarora War, and all were apparently instigated by South Carolina traders. In 1703 and 1706, trader James Child managed to "encourage" two Cherokee raids against Coosa and Tallapoosa towns that netted 160 slaves (Gallay 2002:220; Oatis 2004:53). In 1708, Thomas Nairne brought charges against Child for these raids and accused many of South Carolina's traders of having "contracted a habit . . . [of] inciting one Tribe of our friends to destroy others, merely to purchase the prisoners taken for slaves" (quoted in Gallay 2002:219).

The other example is the well-known and oft-written-about Chestowee raid of 1713, in which a group of Cherokee "cut off" (i.e., utterly routed) the Yuchi town of Chestowee, killing or enslaving most of its inhabitants (Bauxar 1957a, 1957b; Lewis and Kneberg 1946; McDowell 1992:53–57; Riggs 2010). The official inquest held by the Commissioners of the Indian Trade found that the raid was inspired by South Carolina traders Alexander Long and Eleazar Wiggan (McDowell 1992:53–57). Fellow traders among the Yuchi and Cherokee stated that Alexander Long sought out the raid as revenge for an attack he suffered at the hands of some Yuchi. The traders conspired with the headmen of a few Overhill and Middle towns, who agreed to attack Chestowee and sell the slaves captured in the raid to pay off the trading debts they owed to Long and Wiggan.

Joining the Fray: The Yamasee and Creek-Cherokee Wars

Historians have often described the Yamasee War as a watershed event because it marked South Carolina's recognition of Cherokee trading and military potential (Crane 2004:39–41; Hatley 1995:19–22; Oatis 2004:184–186). I would add that the Yamasee War (and more importantly the ensuing Creek-Cherokee War) forced an end to Cherokee isolationism and necessitated sustained social, economic, and political relations between Cherokee groups and South Carolina. From the perspective of the besieged Charlestonians who suffered the agonizing summer of 1715, the Cherokee began the war as a little-known but feared population who were allied with the Yamasee. But after being drawn into the war on the side of South Carolina, the Cherokee were universally hailed as the beloved saviors of the colony. When the details of this Cherokee conversion are considered, however, it becomes apparent that their entrance into the Yamasee War had less to do with helping South Carolina and more to do with going to war with the Creek.

At the outset of the Yamasee War, it is understandable why South Carolina colonists thought the Cherokee were part of a united front against them, but historic accounts demonstrate that only a small minority of Cherokee actually participated in actions against the colonists. During the first weeks of the war, South Carolinians must have felt like the victims of a mass Indian conspiracy when news of the initial Yamasee attacks and the murders of many South Carolinian traders circulated through their settlements. In a letter written in Charleston just days after the war's outbreak, missionary Dr. Francis Le Jau stated: "It appears this Misfortune [was] long since Designed by the General Conspiricy of the Indians that Surround us . . . [Le Jau provides a list of the Indian enemies] very numerous & Potent Towards the North are the Cherikees, the most Potent of all; we depended upon these last, but they are all against us . . . and they have kill'd in cold blood after this Barbarous Mannr such White Men of our own as they could find in their Towns" (Le Jau 1956c [1715]:152). Adding to South Carolinians' suspicions was news that 70 Cherokee joined a party of Catawba in attacking plantations on the Santee River while South Carolinians were still reeling from the first round of attacks (Le Jau 1956d [1715]:158; Rodd 1928 [1715]). These actions, however, comprised the full extent of Cherokee hostility toward South Carolina during the war. Also, the fact that the Cherokee deserted the Catawba war party shortly after they received word that the English sought a peace evinces far less of a commitment to a mass conspiracy than the actions of other hostile groups like the Lower Creek and Apalachee (Eveleigh 1715; Rodd 1928 [1715]).

Perhaps out of desperation, South Carolinians overcame their fear and conducted an ambitious diplomatic mission to make an alliance with the Cherokee. Upon the advice of various Cherokee traders, South Carolina colonial officials held out hope that all Cherokee were not allied with the Yamasee, and with the incentive of a reward of 500 British pounds for success, the colony sent traders Eleazar Wiggan and Robert Gilcrest to seek an alliance (Rodd 1928 [1715]). The traders returned from their mission with eight Cherokee headmen and 120 warriors. With much ceremony, this group of Cherokee declared a peace with South Carolina and agreed to join South Carolina forces in an upcoming mission against the Creek (Le Jau 1956e [1715]:169, 171). South Carolinian jubilation at this alliance quickly turned to uncertainty, however, when the Cherokee failed to join the South Carolina militia at the designated place and time (Crane 2004:180). A diplomatic mission conducted to find out why the Cherokee had not joined the campaign taught two important diplomatic lessons to South Carolinians: that the group of Cherokee who spoke in Charleston did not speak for all Cherokee towns and that factionalism among Cherokee towns would present a constant and formidable obstacle to South Carolina's diplomatic plans for this Indian "nation."

Shortly after the peace ceremonies with the Cherokee were held, Dr. Le Jau (1956e [1715]:169, 171) wrote, "It has Pleasd God to put into the heart of the most Potent Nation that has Sided with our Indian Ennemyes to make a Solemn Peace with us, and Join our Army." For the South Carolinians involved in the diplomatic expedition to hold the Cherokee to their promise, this perception of a unified "nation" of Cherokee coming to the rescue was quickly and thoroughly shattered. The journal kept by Colonel George Chicken (1894 [1715]), one of the leaders of the expedition, documents a much more tenuous and fluid political structure dominated by the autonomous and clashing dispositions of numerous Cherokee headmen.

Upon their arrival among the Cherokee at the Lower Settlements, the expedition was faced with two opposing Cherokee opinions regarding the proposed military alliance against the Yamasee, Creek, and Piedmont Indians. The headman of Tugaloo, known as Charitey Hagey "the Conjuror," assured the South Carolinians that his people no longer held anti-English sentiments. He balked at joining South Carolina's military campaign, however, saying that he could not fight against the Yamasee because "they wer his anchent peapll"; he would not fight against the Creek because they had recently called a truce; and he would not fight the Catawba because he felt they were not to blame for the war (Chicken 1894 [1715]:330). The Conjuror agreed only to fight "ye Sauonose [Savannah] and yutsees [Yuchi] and apolaches [Apalachee]" (Chicken 1894 [1715]:331).

Three days later, Chicken traveled to a nearby town to attend a meeting of headmen who had traveled down from the Middle and Upper settlements. At this meeting, Chicken observed a Cherokee headman named Caesar of Echota vigorously arguing a pro-war position to the assembled audience. Caesar was one of the headmen who made the original promise to aid the South Carolinians at the Charleston peace conference months earlier. His orations appeared to have persuaded many headmen from the Middle and Upper settlements, setting them against the anti-war faction made up of headmen from the Lower Settlements. Hawkish and dovish factions also emerged along generational lines. Chicken (1894 [1715]:331) recorded that the young men, highly motivated by Caesar's speech, began their war ceremonies but were interrupted by "seuerall of their ould men telling them seuerall reasons for them to desist att present." These councils ended with a compromise in which the assembled headmen agreed to "seand ye Ride Stacke [Red Stick] throw the nashon and geatt all Ridey one a day to goe and fitte with ye English" if the Creek did not travel to Tugaloo to settle their tenuous truce with the Cherokee and make peace with the English (Chicken 1894 [1715]:331).

A few weeks later, the hawkish faction from the Middle and Upper settlements threatened to violate the compromise and attack the Creek. Chicken was required to travel to the Upper Settlements in order to delay their attack until he received word of the outcome of the proposed Creek peace talks. The pro-war Cherokee, led by Caesar, would not hear Chicken's pleas and said that they were going to war against the Creek with or without English support. Chicken's (1894 [1715]:342) journal stated, "It was not plunder they [Cherokee] wanted from them [Creek] but to go to war wth them and cut them of, for it was but as yesterday that they were at war together & It was by ye perswasions of ye English they were ever at peace wth them." Caesar thus made it clear that the men among his Cherokee faction were not minions of English diplomacy, and the pro-war headmen left Chicken and marched their assembled host of 2,370 warriors to another settlement in order to prepare for the upcoming raid.

Chicken tried to make his way back to the Lower Settlements in order to head off the approaching Cherokee force, but along the way he received news that the Creek peace delegation had been murdered at Tugaloo. The murders were apparently unlooked for and were not directly related to the events that had just transpired with Caesar and the pro-war faction. Indeed, after the incident rumors abounded that the Cherokee had secretly planned on joining the Creek delegation and a force of 500 Creek warriors in attacking the South Carolina delegation, but they changed their minds at the last minute (Crane 2004:182; Oatis 2004:188). Whatever the motivation, the fallout of the murders was that both the pro- and anti-war factions of the Cherokee were drawn into a war with the Creek, and as an ancillary consequence they entered the Yamasee War on the side of South Carolina.

The murder of the Creek peace delegation in 1716 and the opening of the Creek-Cherokee War has been the focus of much analysis by historians because it was a historical moment that marked a real turning point for South Carolina in the Yamasee War. Indeed, this moment has even been given various titles such as "The Incident at Tugaloo" (Reid 1976:61), "The Massacre at Tugaloo" (Crane 2004:183), and "Salvation at Tugaloo" (Hatley 1995:23). While the Cherokee entrance into a war with the Creek might have meant salvation to South Carolinians, it resulted in over a decade of retaliatory raiding for these Indian adversaries.

The Yamasee War, or more specifically the Incident at Tugaloo, was in fact a major milestone in Cherokee history. From that moment onward, it is clear that the Cherokee could no longer maintain their identity as an "ambiguous presence" in the Appalachian Mountains. As South Carolinians reassessed their colonial strategies during and immediately after the Yamasee War, they recognized the profits they could reap from Cherokee alliance and trade. They subsequently enacted aggressive trading and diplomatic strategies that greatly increased interaction with the Cherokee.

All told, the historic accounts tell a story of dramatic change in Cherokee communities during the English Contact period. Furthermore, these sources demonstrate that this story was unique to the Cherokee and had no direct correlate among other southeastern Indian groups. Until 1715, the Cherokee were but little known to history. From what little was written it appears that they, like most southeastern Indian groups, were weathering the effects of disease, colonial wars, slave raiding, and the deerskin trade. It also appears, however, that the relative isolation of the Cherokee might have offered them some additional measure of refuge from the shatter zone that was not enjoyed by other Indian groups. I would go so far as to argue that Cherokee isolationism was an intentionally enacted strategy used to avoid the turmoil and chaos that wracked other Indian communities—turmoil that was invariably associated with interaction with Europeans.

The murder of the Creek peace delegation in 1716 and the Cherokee's entrance into the Yamasee and Creek-Cherokee wars effectively ended any possibility of maintaining an isolationist strategy. These acts made remaining above the fray impossible for the Cherokee because they awakened both South Carolina's unyielding desire to bring the Cherokee under their aegis and Cherokee communities' need for trade goods to prosecute their war. The resulting sea change in Cherokee strategies can be seen in their meteoric rise to dominate the deerskin trade. In 1708 trade with the Cherokee was described as "inconsiderable," yet a decade later the Cherokee received more trade goods and sent more deerskins to Charleston than all other southeastern Indian groups combined (Marcoux 2008).

Thus far, I have been concerned with delineating the historical context that circumscribes my study of English Contact period Cherokee communities. With this context in place, I can now address the cardinal question of this study: How did ordinary Cherokee households negotiate the turmoil of the English Contact period? I attempt to answer this question by way of an archaeological case study. My interpretations, which are founded upon detailed comparative analyses of pottery assemblages, architecture, and subterranean pit features, focus on characterizing how strategies to cope with the chaos of the shatter zone were inscribed into the material of daily life among households in a Tuckaleechee Town community located in eastern Tennessee—a community manifested in the archaeological record of the Townsend site (40Bt89–40Bt91).

3

The Townsend Site

The Archaeological Embodiment of a Shatter Zone Community

The central case study of my research is the English Contact period Cherokee community manifested in the archaeological record at the Townsend site. The site, which is located along the Little River within Tuckaleechee Cove in eastern Tennessee, contains a collection of architectural features and refuse-filled pits representing the domestic occupation of six widely spaced households. In this chapter, I characterize the physical and cultural geography surrounding the Townsend site and Little River valley. I also assess the ethnohistoric and archaeological evidence associated with Cherokee occupations in the Little River valley. Finally, I describe the excavations at the Townsend site.

PHYSICAL AND CULTURAL GEOGRAPHY SURROUNDING THE LITTLE RIVER VALLEY

The most intriguing aspect of Timberlake's (2001 [1762]) description of Ellejoy (Chapter 1) is that this Cherokee town is located far outside of the region usually attributed to eighteenth-century Cherokee settlements. In fact, with the exception of the town of Watauga, this is the only Cherokee town north of the Little Tennessee River valley mentioned in an existing contemporary account. Timberlake's account raises the question of whether there was a significant Cherokee presence in the Little River valley during the late seventeenth and early eighteenth centuries. If so, this would counter the common perception that few if any permanent Cherokee settlements were located outside of the lower Little Tennessee and Hiwassee river valleys (Schroedl 1986:131).

Anyone who has ever traveled through the traditional Cherokee heartland would quickly acknowledge that a good narrative of Cherokee households and communities must necessarily be rooted in geography, both physical and cultural. Archaeological evidence and contemporary European accounts tell us that during the English Contact period Cherokee communities were spread across three different physiographic provinces: the Piedmont Province of northern South Carolina and Georgia, the Blue Ridge Province of eastern Tennessee and western North Carolina, and the Ridge and Valley Province of eastern Tennessee. That these three provinces correspond to the three settlement divisions recognized by English traders, colonial diplomats, and the Cherokee themselves (the Lower, Middle, and Upper settlements, respectively) is an indicator of the crucial role geography played in Cherokee history.

The majority of the Little River valley lies within the Blue Ridge Province, which encompasses portions of eastern Tennessee, western North Carolina, and extreme northern Georgia. It is a rugged and mountainous region with many peaks possessing maximum elevations of 1,500 m above mean sea level (amsl) or more (Southworth et al. 2005). This province can be divided into highlands and foothills subregions based on general topography. The highlands subregion, which forms the central core of the province, contains the tallest mountains in the southeastern United States (i.e., the Great Smoky Mountains) with elevations that reach over 2,000 m amsl. These peaks form the Eastern Continental Divide, which separates watersheds flowing into the Gulf of Mexico from those flowing to the Atlantic Ocean. The foothills subregion surrounds the highlands subregion and is defined by less extreme slopes with peaks ranging in elevation from 250 to 1,300 m amsl (Southworth et al. 2005). The major river systems draining the Cherokee-occupied portions of the Blue Ridge Province include the Savannah, the French Broad, the Little Tennessee, and the Hiwassee. Once these rivers flow out of the Blue Ridge Province into the Piedmont and Ridge and Valley provinces, they form broad alluvial valleys, but within the province they are narrow and fast moving, offering few areas suitable for large-scale (i.e., greater than household level) agriculture (Dickens 1979, 1986).

There are isolated areas within the Blue Ridge Province that present exceptions to this geographic pattern. These areas, known as *coves* (i.e., Cades Cove, Miller Cove, Wear Cove, and Tuckaleechee Cove), are tectonic windows formed by the erosion of Blue Ridge rocks and the exposure of Ridge and Valley limestone geology (Southworth et al. 2005:49–51) (Figure 3.1). In essence, the coves are small pockets of Ridge and Valley landscape in the midst of the Appalachian Mountains. Topographically these coves feature broad river valleys that are similar to those of the Ridge and Valley Prov-

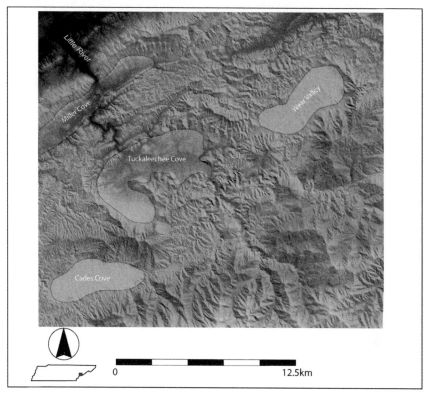

Figure 3.1. Physical geography of the western foothills subregion of the Blue Ridge physiographic province.

ince. These valleys not only possess great potential for agriculture, but they also host a diverse array of plant and animal resources (Bass 1977:7; Braun 1950:201). It is within one of these coves that the Tuckaleechee Towns, including the Townsend site, were settled.

As discussed in Chapter 2, Cherokee communities were largely forsaken by European traders and diplomats until the Yamasee War in 1715. Consequently, there are very few extant records that map out the cultural geography of English Contact period Cherokee communities. Given such a paucity of documents, we are indeed fortunate that one of these records is an extremely detailed map drafted as part of the regionwide Indian census of 1715 (Barnwell 1719; Cumming 1998:Plates 48A and 48D). We can reconstruct a "snapshot" of the region's cultural geography from this map, the Barnwell-Hammerton map, drafted in 1721 (Cumming 1998; Schroedl 2000; Smith 1979). From this map, it is clear that the major English Contact period Cherokee towns were distributed in clusters (Figure 3.2). Annotations on the Barnwell-Hammerton map describe three settlement clusters: those on "this side of the mountains" (i.e., Lower Towns), the "middle settlements" (i.e., the Middle, Valley, and Out towns), and those "beyond the mountains" (i.e., Overhill Towns). These settlement clusters remained stable throughout the eighteenth and early nineteenth centuries (Schroedl 2000; Smith 1979). This apparent stability during the colonial period has led to the common portrayal of these clusters as timeless spatialities. If the historical framework detailed in Chapter 2 applied to the Cherokee, then this stability would be quite anomalous amidst the dynamic backdrop of settlement shifts enacted by other Indian groups during the English Contact period. The Tuckaleechee Towns, located north of the Cherokee settlements depicted in the Barnwell-Hammerton map, present a very important exception to the monolithic portrait of Cherokee settlement patterns—an exception demonstrating that Cherokee communities were indeed fully engaged in the tumultuous emanations of the southeastern shatter zone (Figure 3.2).

The Cherokee towns and settlement divisions were tied together by a series of trails, but trails and rivers also linked Cherokee communities to the wider English Contact period landscape (Dickens 1979; Myer 1928; Ramsey 1999 [1853]; Schroedl 2000). Figure 3.2 shows that all Cherokee settlements were not equally connected to the outside world; instead, trails and rivers offered very different connections for each Cherokee settlement division. The Lower Towns had the most direct access to English traders via trails to Catawba settlements and the Savannah River, but they also were closest to hostile Muskogee-speaking groups—a position that made these communities preferred targets during the Creek-Cherokee War following the Massacre at Tugaloo in 1716. The central location of the Middle, Valley, and Out towns insulated these communities from enemy raids, but this position also limited their contact with European traders vis-à-vis the other settlement divisions. Overhill Towns had greater connections to points west through the Tennessee River and Cumberland trails. These arteries linked Overhill communities to French traders and diplomats as well as enemy Indian groups like the Shawnee and the Illinois. The Tuckaleechee Towns formed the northern extent of Cherokee settlement. While these communities were least well positioned for European trade, being the farthest communities from trails leading to colonial trading centers, they were by no means isolated. Far from being backwater satellite communities deserving of their "forgotten" historical status, the Tuckaleechee Towns were located on a spur off of the Great Indian Warpath, a veritable pedestrian highway that connected Cherokee communities to points north, including the distant Cherokee nemeses the Iroquois. From this brief discussion, it is clear that the variable nature of connections to these various outside groups pre-

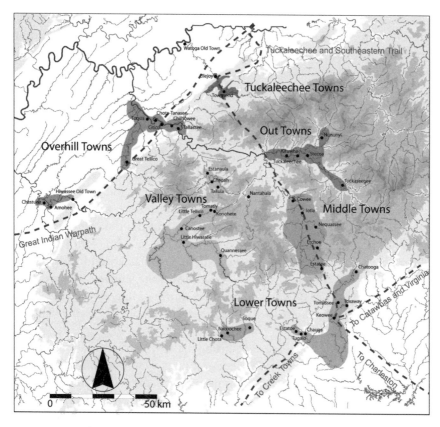

Figure 3.2. Cultural geography of Cherokee territory during the English Contact period (adapted from Duncan and Riggs 2003:Map 3).

sented each Cherokee settlement division with a unique set of opportunities, constraints, and threats.

THE TUCKALEECHEE TOWNS: REDISCOVERING FORSAKEN CHEROKEE COMMUNITIES

Other than Henry Timberlake, nineteenth-century historian James G. M. Ramsey is the only source of information regarding Cherokee settlements in the Little River valley. Ramsey (1999 [1853]:88) mentions Ellejoy and an eponymous creek (Allejay) in his discussion of the Great Indian Warpath. Although very brief, this discussion does provide some very insightful clues about Cherokee occupation of the Little River valley. In his description of the route of the Great Indian Warpath, Ramsey (1999 [1853]:88) speaks of a branching path that leads "to the Tuckaleechee towns, and so on to the Over-hill villages of the Cherokees." While we must be wary of putting too much emphasis on a single statement, I believe that there are two provocative notions contained herein. First is the identification of a group of Cherokee settlements, the "Tuckaleechee towns," in the Little River valley. The second, and perhaps more tenuous, is that these towns are described as a separate settlement division from the Overhill Towns. The question of whether the Tuckaleechee Towns were an autonomous settlement division cannot be answered with the current data, and this will be a very important part of future research in this area. Also, determining when the Tuckaleechee Towns were occupied is impossible because Ramsey is not clear about his historical sources, and this description does not reference any particular time period. One is tempted to believe that Ramsey had access to the personal journal of a Virginia trader, a Mr. Vaughn, who proceeded down the Great Indian Warpath on a trading voyage around 1740 (Ramsey 1999 [1853]:64). Whether Mr. Vaughn was the source of the description will likely never be known, for the majority of Ramsey's personal papers and collections were destroyed when his home was burned during the Civil War.

Cherokee oral history recorded during the nineteenth century adds support to the notion that Cherokee communities were found north of their eighteenth-century homeland at some point in the past. The journal of Major John Norton records this idea in the early nineteenth century. Norton was born to a Cherokee father (from the Lower Town of Keowee) and a Scottish mother. Although Norton was most likely born in Great Britain, he was assigned to a regiment in North America while enlisted in the British army. Eventually, he became an adopted member of an Iroquois town in upstate New York (Klinck 1970:xxv). Norton's journal records a voyage to his ancestral Cherokee homeland in 1813. One of the many conversations with Cherokee elders recorded in Norton's (1970 [1816]:46) journal relays their "earliest traditions" that place "original" Cherokee settlement at the head of the Little Tennessee River.

The personal papers of American actor, editor, and diplomat John Howard Payne relate a similar story of early Cherokee communities. Payne's papers include thousands of pages of Cherokee oral history recorded during a lengthy stay in their settlements and in letters from Cherokee chiefs Charles Hicks and John Ross. In an unpublished volume on Cherokee history Payne penned sometime in the mid-nineteenth century, he (Payne 1814–1841:88) discusses the fact that in earlier times the Cherokee lived near present-day Holston, Tennessee. This purported homeland is indeed far to the north of eighteenth-century Cherokee territory, being closer to Virginia than the

Tuckaleechee Towns. In a letter written to John Ross by Charles Hicks (1826), the Cherokee chief relays a more detailed migration story that places the earliest Cherokee settlements near the headwaters of the Clinch, Cumberland, and Holston rivers in extreme northeastern Tennessee and southwestern Virginia. According to this version of the story, the Cherokee next moved to Noh-nah-cloock-ungh (Na'na-tlu gun'), Nolichucky, or "Spruce-tree place." There is archaeological evidence confirming the existence of early seventeenth-century period Indian settlements located along the present-day Nolichucky River, but excavations at these sites remain unpublished (Smith ca. late 1970s, 1987). Hicks (1826) goes on to say that the Middle, Valley, and Out towns were the first to be settled after the Cherokee left the Nolichucky Valley, followed by the Lower and Overhill towns "many years after." Obviously, this piece of oral history must be assumed to contain the vagaries of time and space that exist in all migration myths. Taking this into account, it is nevertheless significant that multiple sources acknowledge an earlier phase of Cherokee settlement located to the north of their eighteenth-century territory.

The most solid piece of ethnohistoric evidence for Cherokee settlement in the vicinity of the Little River valley is contained in the aforementioned Barnwell-Hammerton map of 1721 (Cumming 1998:Plate 48) and a similar map believed to have been authored by Colonel Barnwell sometime between 1721 and 1724 (called the Barnwell Manuscript map in Cumming 1998:24–25). These maps depict the locations of every known Cherokee town along with the towns of every major Indian group in the Southeast. At the northwestern limits of the Barnwell Manuscript map, just upriver from the confluence of the Little Tennessee River and Tennessee River, is the Watauga River. The Cherokee town of Watauga is depicted at the mouth of the river, which is most likely the present-day Little River. On both maps, the cartographer placed an annotation of "Deserted Settlem." upriver from the mouth of the Watauga River (Figure 3.3). The annotation is unclear as to whether the cartographer was referring to a single settlement or a group of settlements. Regardless, the maps depict the location of the deserted settlement(s) between the "Canot" and "Agihqua" rivers. These were the names given to the West Prong of the Little Pigeon River and the Little Pigeon River, respectively.

Obviously, the static frame offered by these maps can never capture the cultural currents and eddies of the southeastern shatter zone; however, the annotations suggest that the Cherokee were in the process of shifting their settlement patterns during the early English Contact period. Interestingly, the last Cherokee town listed in the 1721 Varnod (1971 [1721]) census is called "Elojay." While there is another town in the list with the

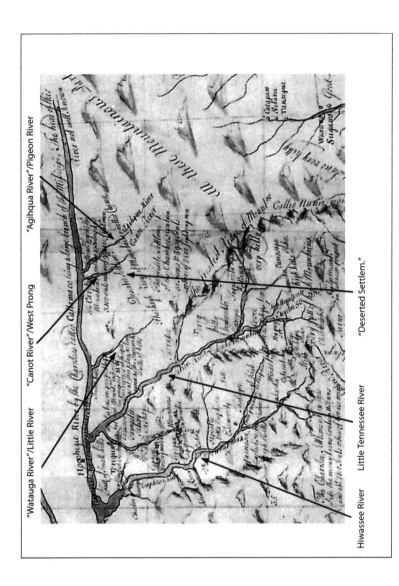

"Watauga River"/Little River   "Canot River"/West Prong   "Agihqua River"/Pigeon River

"Deserted Settlem."

Hiwassee River   Little Tennessee River

Figure 3.3. Magnified view of the 1721 Barnwell-Hammerton map highlighting important land-marks for this study ("Map of part of North America from Cape Charles to the Mouth of the River Mississipi," reproduced in Cumming 1998:Plate 48A–D; original at Yale Center for British Art).

same name, it may be significant that this Elojay is listed among the Over-hill Towns and that no such town has been recorded in the Little Tennes-see or Hiwassee river valleys. The Hunter map (Williams 1928:114) con-firms that the northern settlements (Tuckaleechee Towns) were abandoned by 1730. Considering this together with the two Barnwell maps, we can be reasonably confident that by the time of the Yamasee War, the Cherokee had largely abandoned their northern settlements, including those in the Little River valley, and concentrated their communities southward to the vales of the Little Tennessee and Hiwassee rivers.

THE ARCHAEOLOGY OF THE TUCKALEECHEE TOWNS AND EXCAVATION OF THE TOWNSEND SITE

The Little River valley and surrounding coves have seen precious little professional archaeological attention; however, the few projects that have been conducted in this region point to a significant English Contact period Cherokee occupation within Tuckaleechee Cove. Quentin Bass's (1977) re-port of an archaeological survey of the Great Smoky Mountains National Forest includes two archaeological sites containing Qualla series pottery. One of these sites was located in Cades Cove just south of Tuckaleechee Cove; the other site, which produced a whole simple-stamped jar, was lo-cated near Cosby, Tennessee. Neither of these sites contained European ar-tifacts, and it is difficult to assign the pottery to any archaeological phase based on what is published.

With these exceptions (and the Townsend site), all that is known about the Cherokee occupation of the Little River valley results from a survey con-ducted by Mr. B. Kenneth Cornett, an avocational archaeologist and lifelong resident of Walland, Tennessee (Cornett, personal communication 2007). During the 1960s, Cornett surveyed plowed fields along the lower Little River from Maryville to the entrance of the Great Smoky Mountains Na-tional Forest at the eastern end of Tuckaleechee Cove. During the survey, Cornett identified and made surface collections from 14 sites containing gravel-tempered complicated-stamped and simple-stamped pottery, plain shell-tempered pottery, and glass trade beads. The sites were typically found within 100 m of the river, in the rich alluvial soil of Tuckaleechee Cove. Based on its location at the confluence of Ellejoy Creek and the Little River, one of these sites is believed to be the Cherokee town of Ellejoy (40Bt9) de-scribed by Timberlake (2001 [1762]:118–119) (Figure 3.4). In an interview I conducted with Mr. Cornett, he recalled giving the collections and records from the survey to the McClung Museum at the University of Tennessee. I was able to relocate the original U.S. Geological Survey quadrangles that

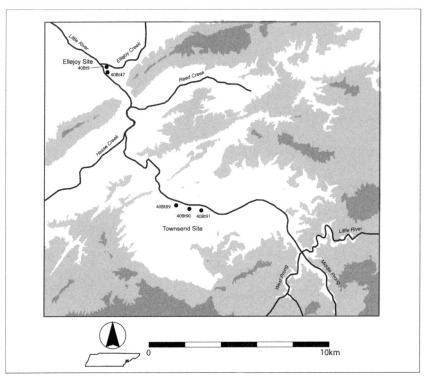

Figure 3.4. Map depicting recorded Cherokee sites in the Little River valley.

contained the site location information from Cornett's survey, but unfortunately I could not turn up any evidence of the artifact collections. In addition to the Townsend site, one other site identified by Cornett has been professionally excavated (40Bt47) (Bentz and Greene 1991). Virtually all of the artifacts and features uncovered during the excavations were associated with an early Mississippian period settlement, but a single turquoise glass necklace bead was found.

The Townsend site (40Bt89–40Bt91) is located in the western portion of Tuckaleechee Cove on a terrace south of the Little River near present-day Townsend, Tennessee (Figure 3.5). The site was originally recorded as three sites (40Bt89–40Bt91) in 1999 as part of a cultural resources survey initiated by the widening of U.S. Highway 321 (Marcoux 2008). In addition to English Contact period Cherokee occupations, the site contained evidence of occupations dating to the Late Archaic through early Mississippian periods (ca. 2500 B.C.–A.D. 1300). Later that year, archaeologists with the Transportation Center at the University of Tennessee, Knoxville, conducted data recovery excavations at the site. These excavations were truly

Figure 3.5. Aerial photograph of excavations at the Townsend site (photograph courtesy of the University of Tennessee Archaeological Research Laboratory).

monumental—on a scale that is rarely seen in post-Depression-era archaeology. Mitigation of the site entailed the use of heavy machinery to strip plow-disturbed soil from the entire site in order to expose subsurface cultural features (e.g., pits, basins, hearths, postholes, burials, etc.). Over the course of the two-year field project, mechanical excavations uncovered over 100,000 m² of the site, resulting in the identification of thousands of features and dozens of structures including two palisaded Mississippian villages, portions of multiple Woodland villages, and the remains of six separate Cherokee households. The Cherokee occupational component at the Townsend site is utterly dwarfed by the earlier occupations, especially those of the Woodland period; however, this small number of archaeological contexts provides a wealth of data regarding the daily lives of English Contact period Cherokee households.

The six Cherokee households at the Townsend site are comprised of structures and pit features distributed widely over the length of the site (Figure 3.6). Available evidence dating the household occupations indicates that they are generally contemporaneous. Radiocarbon dating of samples from features provided spurious results, but archaeomagnetic dating of samples from the hearths of three of these households returned the same date range of ca. 1600–1740 (Lengyel 2004:Table 5.2). Diagnostic glass trade beads and pottery from the site offer a narrower date range, placing the occupation between ca. 1650 and 1720 (Marcoux 2008).

Discussion

In this chapter, I introduced the thesis that the Tuckaleechee Towns were Cherokee communities that were settled in the Little River valley during the late seventeenth and early eighteenth centuries. I provided ethnohistoric and archaeological evidence in support of this thesis. While much more work needs to be done identifying and synthesizing data from other sites in the Little River valley, at this point we can indulge in some informed speculation regarding English Contact period Cherokee settlement patterns in this region. First, the physical and cultural geography surrounding the Tuckaleechee Towns would have presented both advantages and disadvantages to households living in the cove. The unique geology of the cove must have been attractive to Cherokee communities because it offered the benefits of a broad alluvial landscape within a well-protected mountain refuge. Beginning in the early eighteenth century when Iroquois raiding parties began streaming southward, however, Tuckaleechee Cove would have become a dangerous location given its proximity to the Great Indian Warpath

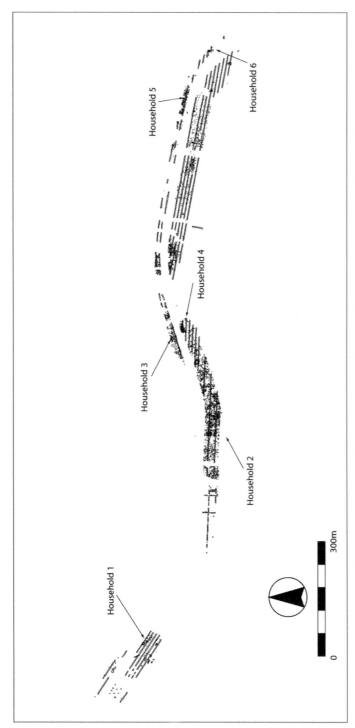

Figure 3.6. Map depicting the locations of the six Cherokee households identified during the Townsend Archaeological Project.

(Norton 1970 [1816]:262). Indeed, these raids may have been a major contributing factor in the choice to abandon the area.

    If only historical sources were consulted, one would assume that Cherokee communities went largely unaffected by the disruptions of the shatter zone until they joined the fray of the Yamasee War in 1715. This conclusion would be even easier to arrive at for the isolated communities located in Tuckaleechee Cove. Fortunately, archaeology allows us to push beyond the dearth of maps and personal accounts that confine our historical understandings of the period to ask, What was life like for the Cherokee families that chose to settle in Tuckaleechee Cove during the late seventeenth century? Were folk in this area spared the disruptions of the shatter zone, or were they instead, through their strategic actions, the very embodiment of the shatter zone? The household contexts at the Townsend site present the perfect case study for analyses that attempt to answer these questions. As units of analysis, data from these households allow us to achieve an incredible level of detail by isolating the daily practices of individual families (e.g., Allison 1999; Lightfoot 2005; Lightfoot et al. 1998; Wesson 2008).

4

Potting Traditions and Household Identities at Townsend

All current archaeological interpretations concerning Cherokee origins, historical development, and daily life are in one way or another founded upon ceramic analyses (e.g., Dickens 1979; Hally 1986a; Riggs and Rodning 2002; Rodning 2004; Schroedl 1986). In this chapter, I apply a number of quantitative attribute analyses to ceramic data from the Townsend site and other Cherokee sites in order to construct a culture history for the English Contact period. These analyses extend the traditional definition of culture history by presupposing that the production of pottery vessels was a socially meaningful practice that was essential for creating shared household identities. Through these analyses, I identify three analytically distinct potting traditions among the Cherokee households at Townsend. One of the potting traditions has clear ties to the lower Little Tennessee River valley; one has ties to western North Carolina and northern Georgia; and one tradition most likely represents a local phenomenon with no known antecedent. I argue that the presence of these distinct potting traditions at Townsend indicates that this settlement was an improvised coalescent community (*sensu* Kowalewski 2006) of families that immigrated to Tuckaleechee Cove from disparate parts of Cherokee territory sometime during the latter half of the seventeenth century.

THE OVERHILL AND QUALLA CERAMIC SERIES

The Overhill and Qualla pottery series are taxonomic systems that were created in order to identify and classify geographic and temporal variability among historic and prehistoric Cherokee pottery assemblages (Baden 1983;

Bates 1986; Egloff 1967; Hally 1986a; Keel 1976; Lewis and Kneberg 1946; Lewis et al. 1995; Riggs and Rodning 2002; Rodning 2004; Ward and Davis 1999; Wilson and Rodning 2002). The most obvious differences between the two series involve the types of aplastic materials used as tempering agents in vessel construction and the types of surface treatments applied to vessel exteriors. These differences are often summarized by saying that Overhill series vessels were tempered with crushed mussel shell and had smoothed or scraped exterior surfaces while Qualla series vessels were tempered with grit and had carved paddle–stamped exterior surfaces. The repetition of this statement has resulted in the common belief that these series reflect clear differences in long-held traditions practiced by potters in Overhill Cherokee settlements, on the one hand, and those in the Middle, Valley, Out Town, and Lower settlements on the other (Dickens 1979; Egloff 1967; Schroedl, ed. 1986).

However, the Overhill and Qualla ceramic series must also be seen as the products of two separate long-term Cherokee research projects at the University of Tennessee and the University of North Carolina. The research conducted by University of Tennessee archaeologists focused on historically documented mid-eighteenth-century Overhill Cherokee communities in the lower Little Tennessee River valley and resulted in large data sets covering a very narrow time span. The research of archaeologists at the University of North Carolina, by contrast, was focused on large-scale regional surveys among the Middle, Valley, and Out Town settlements and excavations aimed at characterizing the long-term chronological development of Cherokee communities in western North Carolina. This work resulted in smaller data sets with relatively great geographic breadth and temporal depth (ca. A.D. 1300–1908 for the Qualla series versus ca. A.D. 1700–1838 for the Overhill series) but with little eighteenth-century coverage (Figure 4.1). Consequently, one must be careful not to mistakenly attribute differences between these ceramic series to differences in potting traditions of equal time depth.

The Overhill Ceramic Series

The first formal description of Overhill Cherokee pottery was penned by Lewis and Kneberg (1946:98–99; Lewis et al. 1995:117) in their classic works on the Hiwassee Island site excavations and the Chickamauga Basin survey. These initial descriptions of Overhill Cherokee pottery were interesting for several reasons. First, Lewis and Kneberg's descriptions of Overhill pottery only covered shell- and grit-tempered sherds with check-stamped and

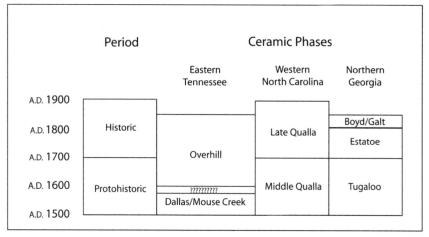

Period		Ceramic Phases		
		Eastern Tennessee	Western North Carolina	Northern Georgia
A.D. 1900				
A.D. 1800	Historic		Late Qualla	Boyd/Galt
				Estatoe
A.D. 1700		Overhill		
A.D. 1600	Protohistoric	??????????? Dallas/Mouse Creek	Middle Qualla	Tugaloo
A.D. 1500				

Figure 4.1. Ceramic chronology for Cherokee pottery assemblages.

complicated-stamped surfaces. They did not include shell-tempered sherds with smoothed surfaces (i.e., plain), which later came to be known as a diagnostic hallmark of the Overhill series. This omission was most likely due to the fact that plain shell-tempered Overhill series body sherds were (and still are) indistinguishable from those associated with the earlier Mississippian period. Also, even though Lewis and Kneberg's descriptions of Overhill pottery appeared in the reports for Hiwassee Island and the Ocoee site, they were not based on the pottery assemblages recovered from these sites. The Hiwassee Island assemblage contained three possible Overhill sherds and the Ocoee site assemblage included approximately 30 rims with notched rimstrips and 30 complicated-stamped body sherds. Instead, Lewis and Kneberg formulated their descriptions of Overhill pottery from samples excavated at the sites of Chota and Fort Loudon, the latter being a mid-eighteenth-century English trading fort located in the lower Little Tennessee River valley.

It appears that the primary reason the authors included these descriptions in the Hiwassee Island and Chickamauga Basin reports was to present their model for Cherokee origins. Drawing attention to the similarities between the paddle-stamped wares found at Fort Loudon and those at other historically known Cherokee settlements like the Peachtree site (Little Hiwassee), Nacoochee, Kituhwa, Nununyi, and Nequassee, Lewis and Kneberg (1946:98) put forth the argument that the Cherokee were an intrusive group of immigrants that entered western North Carolina and eastern Tennessee in historic times, replacing local Muskogee-speaking Mississippian groups. The replacement, they argued, was supported archaeologically by the apparent replacement of plain, cord-marked, and incised shell-tempered pottery with check-stamped and complicated-stamped pottery.

Brian Egloff's (1967) research provided a large leap forward in understanding historic Cherokee pottery, particularly in linking the geographic distribution of plain shell-tempered pottery with the Overhill Cherokee. The goal of Egloff's study was to examine the variability among pottery assemblages from a number of different Cherokee sites. Egloff's study included samples from sites in each of the five historically documented Cherokee settlement divisions (i.e., Overhill, Middle, Valley, Out Town, and Lower). Surface collections from the eastern Tennessee sites of Citico and Great Tellico composed the Overhill Cherokee portion in the study. While this study did not adequately consider time as a source of variability among pottery assemblages, it nevertheless succeeded in recognizing that the majority of Overhill Cherokee pottery was shell tempered with plain surfaces and that this pottery was largely restricted to sites located west of the Appalachian Summit, occurring only in very small frequencies among the other Cherokee settlement divisions (Egloff 1967:43–44, 73).

By far the largest contribution to the development of the Overhill ceramic series came as part of the Tellico Archaeological Project. This project, carried out by archaeologists at the University of Tennessee, included a survey of the lower Little Tennessee River valley and excavations at numerous sites prior to the construction of the Tellico Dam. Between the late 1960s and the late 1970s, excavations were carried out at a number of Overhill Cherokee towns documented in Lieutenant Henry Timberlake's journal and map drafted in 1762. These towns included Citico, Chota-Tanasee, Mialoquo, Tomotley, Toqua, and Tuskegee (Baden 1983; Chapman 1979; Guthe and Bistline 1981; Polhemus 1987; Russ and Chapman 1983; Schroedl, ed. 1986). The Tellico Archaeological Project excavations expanded the corpus of Overhill pottery from a few thousand sherds to well over 500,000 sherds (King 1977:154–155). This large sample allowed for analyses at an unprecedented scale, including studies of Overhill vessel forms (King 1977) and more detailed descriptions of surface treatments and rimstrip morphology (Baden 1983; Bates 1986; Russ and Chapman 1983).

Since little research regarding the Overhill ceramic series has been conducted in recent years, the following description draws upon the primary sources of the Tellico Archaeological Project (Baden 1983:37–62; Bates 1986: 289–305; King 1977; Russ and Chapman 1983:69–83). It is imperative to keep in mind that these sources report on Overhill pottery assemblages primarily associated with the English Colonial and Revolutionary War periods (1740–1794). As presented in these reports, the Overhill ceramic series is dominated by plain shell-tempered pottery with minority surface treatments including (in order of typical frequency) check stamping, simple stamping, complicated stamping, incising, cob marking or roughening, and cord marking.

Unfortunately, vessel forms were not reported consistently in the various Tellico project publications. Neither Bates (1986) nor Russ and Chapman (1983) provides detailed discussions of Overhill vessel form or tallies of different vessel forms in their reports on the Chota-Tanasee and Mialoquo excavations. King (1977) collaborated with a number of contemporary Cherokee speakers and noted potter Amanda Swimmer in an innovative attempt to define vessel classes for the Tellico Archaeological Project Overhill pottery assemblages. Combining data recorded from whole vessels with suggestions provided by his collaborators, King (1977) came up with 10 vessel classes for the Overhill series, including small bowls, medium bowls, wide shallow bowls with flaring rims, wide slightly deeper bowls with less flaring rims, large cazuelas and hemispherical bowls, small globular jars, medium globular jars, large globular jars, very shallow flat-bottomed pans or plates, and medium-sized flat-bottomed pans. At the site of Tomotley, Baden (1983:57) utilized a much less detailed vessel classification system and reported that jars were by far the most abundant vessel form, followed by hemispherical bowls, flat-bottomed pans, and cazuelas.

Another diagnostic attribute of Overhill series vessels is a coil of clay added around the entire circumference of a vessel just below the lip or shoulder. These decorative additions, known collectively as "rimstrips," are typically either modeled from the final vessel coil, by folding, or applied as a separate coil, by a technique known as "filleting." Various decorative techniques were applied to rimstrips, including finger pinching, punctating, and notching with a sharp stylus. Such variability suggests that differences in rimstrip decoration may be associated with different vessel forms or that these decorative techniques may be temporally sensitive. Like vessel form, there is little consistency in how rimstrip decoration was recorded in the various Tellico Archaeological Project reports. The impression one gets from the reports, however, is that stylus notching is much more frequent than either pinching or punctating in the mid- to late eighteenth-century assemblages.

The Qualla Ceramic Series

In contrast to the temporally and geographically restricted Overhill ceramic series, the Qualla ceramic series was constructed with data from regional surveys and excavations at a number of historic and prehistoric sites in western North Carolina. Consequently, it offers a much broader culture history framework. Indeed, in 40 years of research in western North Carolina, archaeologists have been able to demonstrate that the Qualla ceramic series represents a 500-year-long South Appalachian pottery tradition (Egloff 1967; Hally 1986a, 1994; Keel 1976; Riggs and Rodning 2002; Rodning 2004; Ward and Davis 1999; Wilson and Rodning 2002). Thorough histories of the development of this ceramic series can be found in other works (Marcoux 2008; Riggs and Rodning 2002; Rodning 2004); therefore, here I limit my discussion to the most current description of Qualla.

Rodning (2004) and Riggs (Riggs and Rodning 2002; Shumate et al. 2005) have done much to refine the Qualla ceramic series by identifying fine-grained diachronic patterns of change involving surface treatment, vessel form, and rimstrip morphology. After considering the radiocarbon dates calculated for features at the Coweeta Creek site in western North Carolina, Rodning (2004:312) made slight alterations to the calendrical date ranges assigned to the three Qualla phases originally defined by Ward and Davis (1999). Rodning's (2004:312) new phase ranges include the Early Qualla phase (ca. A.D. 1300–1500), the Middle Qualla phase (ca. A.D. 1500–1650), and the Late Qualla phase (ca. A.D. 1650–1838). Middle and Late Qualla phase pottery is essentially identical to pottery associated with the Tugaloo and Estatoe phases (seventeenth- and eighteenth-century occupations at sites in the Lower Cherokee settlement division) in northeast Georgia (Hally 1986a; Riggs and Rodning 2002:38).

The portion of the ceramic series related to the Early Qualla phase was defined by assemblages recovered from the Cherokee Casino site and the Coweeta Creek site (Riggs et al. 1997; Rodning 2004). These assemblages contain both curvilinear and rectilinear complicated-stamped surface treatments, with the latter tending to be more numerous. Less numerous but highly diagnostic Early Qualla phase surface treatments include diamond check stamping, red filming, and wiping that resulted in the extrusion of temper particles to the vessel surface (called coarse plain). Sherds having a compact sandy paste, rimstrips with sawtooth notching, and unmodified rims (i.e., lacking rimstrips) are also highly diagnostic of this subphase (Riggs and Rodning 2002:39; Rodning 2004:314). Early Qualla vessel assemblages contain everted-rim jars with and without rimstrips, tall-neck jars with unmodified rims (resembling late Savannah phase jars), and small red-filmed bowls with simple incised motifs. Incised cazuelas are rare.

Middle Qualla phase ceramic assemblages are dominated by curvilinear and rectilinear complicated-stamped surface treatments. During this subphase, however, curvilinear motifs including scrolls (so-called figure nines and figure Ps), concentric circles, keyholes, and wavy lines are much more

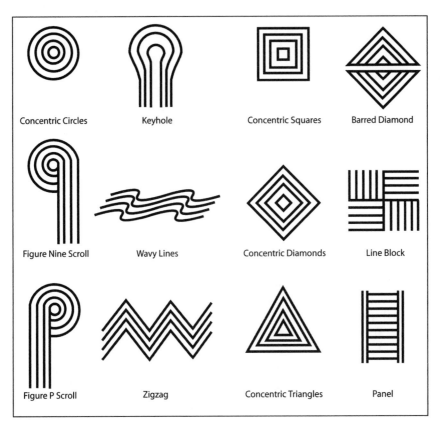

Figure 4.2. Stamped motifs applied to Overhill series and Qualla series vessels.

frequent (Figure 4.2). Minority surface treatments include cord marking, smoothing (i.e., plain), and cob roughening, and Middle Qualla phase assemblages lack the distinctive diamond check stamping of the previous subphase (Rodning 2004:314). Also, incising becomes a much more prevalent surface treatment during the Middle Qualla phase, with both curvilinear and rectilinear motifs being present (Figure 4.3) (Riggs and Rodning 2002:43–44). The increase in incising as a surface treatment was due to a dramatic increase in the frequency of the cazuela vessel form in Middle Qualla phase assemblages. This vessel form has a sharply carinated profile featuring complicated stamping beneath the shoulder and incising above. Middle Qualla phase vessel assemblages also include jars with highly everted rims and pinched and flattened rimstrips, as well as small restricted-orifice hemispherical bowls with folded and punctated rims (Shumate et al. 2005:6. 10–6.11).

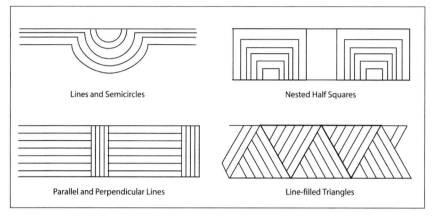

Figure 4.3. Incised motifs applied to Overhill series and Qualla series vessels.

Rectilinear complicated stamping, particularly featuring panel and line block motifs, and square check stamping become dominant surface treatments during the Late Qualla phase (Riggs and Rodning 2002:45). Incising is present in much-diminished frequencies early in the subphase, and this surface treatment virtually disappears from Qualla assemblages along with the cazuela form after the mid-eighteenth century (Rodning 2004:312). Jar forms of the Late Qualla subphase have excurvate rather than highly everted rims, and they feature much more prominent coronal rimstrips. These rimstrips are more often stylus notched than pinched and flattened (Rodning 2004:312). By the late eighteenth century, Qualla vessel assemblages also include significant numbers of medium and large flat-bottomed pans (Riggs and Rodning 2002:45).

Implications for Studying the Townsend Pottery Assemblage

With the exception of Egloff's (1967) research, the historical developments of the Overhill and Qualla ceramic series have proceeded separately. These separate research histories have greatly impacted the way pottery has been related to the history and prehistory of Cherokee communities—especially Overhill communities. As a result of the isolated nature of Cherokee research, Middle, Valley, Out Town, and Lower Cherokee settlement divisions currently appear as a coherent group whose deep regional histories are evinced in the half-millennium-long Qualla series (Riggs and Rodning 2002; Rodning 2004). Overhill communities, on the other hand, appear enigmatic because their style of potting is so different from that of Qualla (i.e., shell tempered with plain surfaces) and because this style is not manifested in an unbroken regional ceramic sequence spanning multiple centuries. In terms of temper (i.e., shell), surface treatment (i.e., plain), and basic vessel form, Overhill assemblages are similar to the wares of the preceding Dallas and Mouse Creek phases in eastern Tennessee; however, the temporal distribution of these two prehistoric phases only extends into the late sixteenth century. This leaves an apparent gap in material culture assemblages spanning the entire seventeenth century—a gap that has fueled the debates over the origins of the Overhill Cherokee in eastern Tennessee (Dickens 1979; Schroedl 1986; Schroedl, ed. 1986:533). Fortunately, the pottery assemblage from the Townsend site directly addresses this gap.

What has not been considered is the possibility that components of the Overhill ceramic series spanning this gap exist but that these components were stylistically different from earlier sixteenth-century assemblages *and* later eighteenth-century assemblages. Such consideration would logically include entertaining the possibility that earlier Overhill series pottery assemblages were much more diverse than middle to late eighteenth-century assemblages and that these earlier Overhill assemblages were in some ways similar to contemporaneous Qualla series assemblages. The Cherokee pottery assemblage recovered from the Townsend site represents just such a scenario. Indeed, the results of the analyses described below demonstrate that the potting traditions practiced in these late seventeenth- and early eighteenth-century households were not nearly as homogenous as they were in the mid-eighteenth century. The results also refute the implicit notion that the potting traditions represented by the Overhill and Qualla series remained geographically isolated until the large-scale refugee migrations associated with the American Revolutionary War (Baden 1983:148–149; Bates 1986:322; Russ and Chapman 1983:82–83).

Pottery Production and the Materialization of Household Identity at Townsend

There are a number of reasons the Townsend pottery sample is critically important to our understanding of English Contact period Cherokee communities. First, the sample of Cherokee pottery recovered from the Townsend excavations represents the only relatively large and well-studied pottery assemblage from a Cherokee community located north of the Little Tennessee River valley, a region where little research into Cherokee communities has been conducted. Second, the pottery sample from the Townsend site and a small sample from the Ocoee site in the Hiwassee River valley together make up the only Overhill Cherokee pottery assemblages thought to date to the late seventeenth and early eighteenth centuries. Third, the

Townsend pottery sample is important because it differs dramatically from later Overhill Cherokee assemblages.

The main challenge one has to confront when conducting an archaeological study of identity is how to make this rather ethereal theoretical notion into an empirical phenomenon. Within the past half century researchers of culture have devised many ways to grapple with the notion of identity as it relates to community (e.g., Barth 1969; Boyd and Richerson 1987; Lincoln 1989; Roosens 1989). While "identity" has been problematized and theorized in many very different ways, a couple of points can be observed that are common to all. First, identities in communities seem to be related to distinctions of sameness and difference (i.e., "us" and "them") and, second, identities are tied to performance—they are phenomena that people must enact in order to maintain (Callon 1986; Latour 1991, 1992, 1999, 2005; Law 1999; Roosens 1989; Salamone and Swanson 1979). Given these two points, it seems logical that scholars of the past decade have chosen to cast their studies of identity in the terms of theories that stress human action (often called *practice*) and the discourses that result (Bourdieu 1977; Giddens 1979; Lincoln 1989).

In the field of archaeology, attention has recently been placed on identifying the processes of identity construction by relating theories of human action to the archaeological record through the notion of materiality (e.g., Dietler and Herbich 1998; Dobres 2000; Hodder and Cessford 2004; Sinclair 2000; Wesson 2008). Behind the concept of materiality is the idea that while an individual's identity is extremely flexible and transient, it (or aspects of it) can be made a "historical fact" through material media such as objects or use of space (Chilton 1999; Joyce and Hendon 2000:154; Yaeger and Canuto 2000:7). Because the notion of materiality allows researchers to consider material culture as both a reflection and an active instrument of identity construction, it brings empirical study into the often too ethereal discussions of practice in archaeology (Conkey 1999; Pauketat 2000b, 2001). Returning to the question of how to relate identity to archaeological data (or how to give substance to the gossamer wings of a "notion"), I argue that the key challenge in characterizing practices related to identity construction is determining how that action contributed to creating an "us" and "them" distinction either within a single community or among communities. Specifically, I identify these distinctions by focusing on the various choices potters were confronted with while making a pot. This requires a technological study of pottery inspired by the analytical technique known as *chaînes opératoires*.

Archaeologists researching Paleolithic technologies have employed the methodology known as *chaînes opératoires* to explore how individuals might have constructed their identities through both nondiscursive and discursive practices (although the former type of practice is almost always implicated) (e.g., Dietler and Herbich 1998; Dobres 2000; Sinclair 2000; Stark 1998; van der Leeuw 1993). This methodology is derived from the French *technologie* school of thought (Lemonnier 1993). This school established the idea that technologies are reflective of the fact that human behavior consists of deeply embedded operational sequences. The *chaînes opératoires* offers the analyst a way to "map" the manufacture of a technology as a sequence of stages, each of which presents a series of choices to the producer. Linking this method to theories of action involves identifying and understanding the factors that condition the choices made at each stage of production. Most researchers using this method evoke *habitus* (Bourdieu 1977) or Giddensian *structure* (Giddens 1979) when discussing the conditioning of choices. Indeed, these concepts provide very good ways of conceptualizing the "durable dispositions" that are created through recursive daily technological practices, dispositions that ultimately influence perceptions of the possibilities that exist to the producer. In this way, the analyst can understand technology as a meaningful act of social engagement with the material world through which knowledge as well as things were produced and reproduced.

I adapt the *chaînes opératoires* method to the pottery-making technologies in late seventeenth- and early eighteenth-century Cherokee communities (see Dietler and Herbich 1998 for an ethnoarchaeological example addressing pottery making). Breaking down the various decision-making stages of manufacture, I identify the attributes that result from these decisions. Based on the findings and critiques of recent scholars, these attributes reflect not just decoration but a combination of technology (i.e., pottery ware), decoration (i.e., surface treatment), and form (i.e., vessel form) (e.g., Dietler and Herbich 1998; Dobres 2000; Hegmon 1998). Cherokee potters at Townsend chose the raw materials from which they made their pots. These choices included clay source, type of aplastic tempering agent, temper particle size, and the amount of tempering agent used. These choices are manifested in pottery ware attributes. Cherokee potters typically built up vessels from a series of coils using a wooden paddle. In doing so, the potters chose from a variety of treatments applied to the exterior of the vessel. The major choice in surface treatment faced by Townsend potters was between a plain surface and one of a number of stamped designs that were either carved into the paddle or made by wrapping cordage around the paddle. One of the most observable choices made by Townsend potters concerned vessel form. Townsend potters made a variety of vessels for daily use in households, including globular jars, bowls, and cazuelas. In my analysis, I search for patterns in the combinations of these attribute states that likely reflect similarities and differences in choices made by household potters. I also explore the spatial distributions of the attributes. The extent to which household or community-level identities are recursively produced through pottery manufacture should be evident in these spatial distributions.

Pottery Ware

The technological foundations of what I believe are the three potting traditions practiced by Townsend household potters are materialized as three distinct pottery wares found among Townsend household pottery assemblages. Differences among these wares are evident in four attributes including (1) the type of aplastic material used to temper the clay bodies of vessels, (2) the size of tempering agent particles, (3) the density of the tempering agent used in the paste, and (4) the thickness of vessel walls.

The most readily observable difference among the three pottery wares involves the types of aplastic materials used as tempering agents in vessel construction (Table 4.1). The most common tempering agent found in the Townsend pottery sample consists of a mixture of metaigneous and other rock types, primarily quartz, quartzite, feldspar, and muscovite-schist. The round shape of the particles in this ware group is reminiscent of water-worn gravel, suggesting that this tempering material was gathered from the nearby banks of the Little River (Figure 4.4, top).

Crushed mussel shell comprises the second most common tempering agent used in Cherokee pottery at Townsend. In all but a few instances, the shell particles have leached out of the sherd, leaving a highly porous clay body (Figure 4.4, center). Without the presence of the actual tempering agent, classification in these cases relies on the lenticular arrangement of the voids throughout the paste—an unmistakable hallmark of shell tempering.

A minority of sherds in the sample are tempered with various types of igneous and metaigneous rock particles, primarily quartz. This tempering agent, known as grit, conforms to the typical definition of the Qualla series (see also Shumate et al. 2005:6.5). Grit differs from gravel primarily in particle shape (angular not round). The paste of this ware is also much more micaceous than that of the gravel-tempered or shell-tempered ware groups (Figure 4.4, bottom). The mica flecks contained in these sherds are probably natural inclusions and not intentional, suggesting that grit-tempered vessels were constructed using clay from a source or sources other than those used in making gravel- and shell-tempered wares. The similarity of this ware to that of Qualla series sherds found among the Middle, Valley,

Figure 4.4. Tempering material in the Townsend pottery
assemblage. Top, gravel; center, shell; bottom, grit.

Table 4.1. Cherokee body sherd assemblage recovered from the Townsend excavations

Temper	Exterior Surface Treatment	n	%
Gravel			
	Plain	881	20.29
	Indeterminate linear stamped	714	16.44
	Indeterminate stamped	502	11.56
	Coarse plain	476	10.96
	Cord marked	407	9.37
	Eroded	259	5.96
	Curvilinear complicated stamped	134	3.09
	Scraped	56	1.29
	Complicated stamped	48	1.11
	Burnished	27	.62
	Simple stamped	26	.60
	Cob roughened	25	.58
	Incised	11	.25
	Brushed	10	.23
	Fingernail punctated	1	.02
	Stylus punctated	1	.02
	Rectilinear complicated stamped	1	.02
	Total	3,579	82.41
Shell			
	Plain	360	8.29
	Eroded	83	1.91
	Scraped	54	1.24
	Burnished	5	.12
	Cob roughened	3	.07
	Indeterminate linear stamped	2	.05
	Cord marked	1	.02

Temper	Exterior Surface Treatment	n	%
	Fingernail punctated	1	.02
	Red filmed	1	.02
	Total	510	11.74
Grit			
	Indeterminate linear stamped	92	2.12
	Plain	55	1.27
	Indeterminate stamped	28	.64
	Curvilinear complicated stamped	25	.58
	Complicated stamped	9	.21
	Eroded	9	.21
	Burnished	8	.18
	Coarse plain	6	.14
	Scraped	4	.09
	Cord marked	3	.07
	Brushed	3	.07
	Check stamped	2	.05
	Incised	1	.02
	Total	245	5.64
Shell and gravel			
	Plain	3	.07
	Indeterminate stamped	2	.05
	Coarse	1	.02
	Cord marked	1	.02
	Indeterminate linear stamped	1	.02
	Scraped	1	.02
	Total	9	.21
Total		4,343	100.00

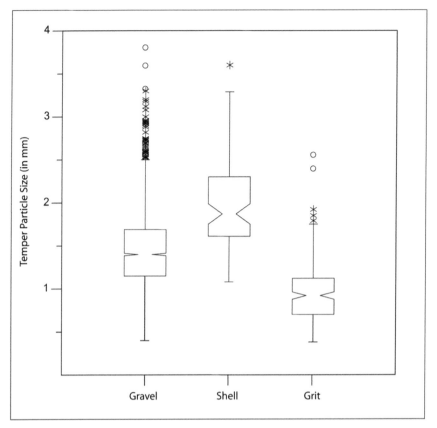

Figure 4.5. Boxplots comparing the distribution of temper particle size among the three Cherokee pottery ware groups.

and Out Town settlement divisions to the east also raises the possibility that the grit-tempered sherds at Townsend may represent vessels made elsewhere. That these three tempering agents were the focus of real choices made by Townsend potters in creating three different pottery wares is attested to by the fact that only nine sherds in the sample contain a mixture of tempers (Table 4.1).

Townsend potters also appear to have made distinctions in the size of the temper particles they used in each of the three pottery wares. The distributions of temper particle diameters are portrayed using a visual display known as a notched boxplot (see Appendix A for a discussion of this statistical display technique) (McGill et al. 1978; Velleman and Hoaglin 1981:65–81). A comparison of the temper particle diameters using notched boxplots reveals statistically significant differences among all three pottery wares (Figure 4.5). The shell-tempered ware has the largest temper particles (n = 510, median = 1.85 mm), followed by gravel-tempered ware (n = 3,579, median = 1.40 mm) and grit-tempered ware (n = 245, median = .92 mm). Indeed, the differences among the ware groups are so great that their H-spreads barely overlap.

There are also appreciable differences among the three wares with regard to the density of temper particles in the clay body. The most accurate quantitative method for this type of comparison would involve point counting temper particles in thin-section slides under a low-power microscope, a method that neither time nor money would allow. As an alternative basis for comparison along this dimension, I employ published visual estimation charts of temper particle density (Matthew et al. 1997:215–263; Orton et al. 1993:Figure A.4). While not as rigorous as petrologic analysis, visual estimation charts nevertheless provide a reasonably objective basis for comparison. In the Townsend pottery sample, gravel-tempered and shell-tempered sherds have similar density values ranging between 20 and 35 percent. The density values of grit-tempered sherds are significantly lower—10 to 20 percent.

Some degree of difference is also apparent among the ware groups in terms of the thickness of vessel walls. This measurement is taken along the midline of each body sherd in the sample. Sherds exhibiting spalling or significant erosion are not included in the analysis. The results of a comparison using notched boxplots indicate that the median sherd thickness of the gravel-tempered ware (n = 3,330, median = 7.6 mm) is significantly greater than that of the shell-tempered ware (n = 475, median = 7.04 mm) and the grit-tempered ware (n = 237, median = 7.08 mm) (Figure 4.6). The median sherd thickness measures of the latter two groups are essentially identical.

Exterior Surface Treatment

The Townsend pottery sample exhibits a number of different exterior surface treatments (Figure 4.7). The most common exterior surface treatment in the Townsend sample is plain (Table 4.1). Following the convention set by other researchers, in this study I make the distinction between three forms of plain surface treatment: plain, burnished, and coarse plain (Hally 1986a, 1994; Rodning 2004). Plain sherds have matte exterior surfaces and often feature very small striations resulting from the dragging of temper particles during the smoothing process (Figure 4.7a). These striations suggest that smoothing took place while the vessel was still fairly wet rather than at a leather-hard stage. Burnished sherds exhibit polished surfaces that have been rubbed with a very smooth-surfaced tool (such as a bone or river pebble) and wiped with a piece of cloth or hide when the vessel was leather hard. In

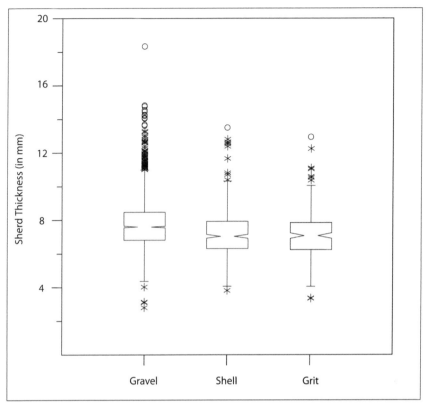

Figure 4.6. Boxplots comparing the distribution of sherd thickness among the three Cherokee pottery ware groups.

order to be categorized as burnished, sherds must reflect light. Coarse plain is a surface treatment category that includes sherds with bumpy exterior surfaces that are "dotted with protruding temper particles" (Figure 4.7b) (Hally 1986a:108). As with burnishing, it appears that Townsend potters achieved this effect by wiping the exterior surface of a vessel with a piece of cloth or hide. Unlike burnishing, in which a potter wipes the exterior of a leather-hard vessel, drawing fine clay particles to the surface in order to achieve a polished appearance, in creating a coarse surface, a potter wipes a wet vessel in order to remove clay particles from the exterior, leaving a rough surface studded with extruded temper particles. That this was an intentional practice is supported by the fact that the interior surfaces of many coarse plain sherds are smoothed or even burnished.

There has been little consistency in the way that carved paddle–stamped pottery has been recorded and analyzed in Cherokee pottery assemblages.

Figure 4.7. Exterior surface treatments and decorative rim modes in the Townsend pottery sample. a, Plain globular jar with pinched rimstrip; b, coarse plain globular jar with smoothed rimstrip; c, indeterminate linear-stamped globular jar with pinched and flattened rimstrip; d, curvilinear complicated-stamped (wavy lines motif) globular jar with pinched and flattened rimstrip; e, cord-marked globular jar with stylus-notched rimstrip; f, incised (line-filled triangles motif) cazuela with unmodified rim.

Because this surface treatment comprises such a large percentage of many Cherokee assemblages and because variability in this surface treatment appears to be temporally sensitive, these differences in classification method can become serious impediments to constructing a robust Cherokee ceramic chronology.

The major differences among current classification methods result from the way each method deals with the fact that the entire design field of a carved paddle is often not present on a single sherd. For example, how does one classify a sherd that features a stamped impression consisting solely of parallel lines? In one classification system, this sherd would be classified as simple stamped (e.g., Baden 1983:53; Bates 1986:300; Russ and Chapman 1983:80); in another system, it would be called rectilinear complicated stamped (Smith et al. 1988:54); and in yet another classification system, it would be called linear stamped (Rodning 2004:271). Given that the relative percentages of sherds bearing curvilinear complicated-stamped motifs and rectilinear complicated-stamped motifs change through time, these three classificatory schemas will likely give different chronological estimates to the same assemblage. Recognizing the promise of carved paddle–stamped pottery to be a powerful component in constructing ceramic chronologies, I argue for a classificatory system that strives for the greatest specificity while at the same time acknowledging the fragmentary nature of potsherd samples.

Fortunately, this system has already been developed and employed by Riggs (Shumate et al. 2005) and Rodning (2004). Theirs is a hierarchical classification system for carved paddle–stamped pottery that can be thought of as progressing from least to most specific given the size and surface conditions of each sherd. The least specific group in the system is called *indeterminate stamped.* This group consists of sherds exhibiting evidence of being stamped with carved wooden paddles but whose surfaces had been smoothed over or were otherwise modified, precluding the identification of any decorative pattern (e.g., check stamped, simple stamped, complicated stamped).

Moving up the hierarchy, the next group is called *indeterminate linear stamped.* Sherds belonging to this group bear the impressions of a series of straight parallel lines (2–5 mm in width) formed by the lands and grooves of a carved wooden paddle. These lines could have been part of a paddle carved solely with a series of straight parallel lines (i.e., simple stamped), or they might represent a portion of a complex rectilinear or curvilinear motif (Figure 4.7c). Because the fragmentary nature of the sherds makes distinguishing among these motifs impossible, analytically these sherds are all considered to be part of the same group. Along with plain sherds, indeterminate linear-stamped sherds make up the majority of the Townsend pottery assemblage (Table 4.1).

The next category, called *complicated stamped*, includes sherds that bear impressions of multiple adjoining lines whose junctures form distinct angles. In this case, the analyst knows that the potter used a paddle bearing a complex motif; however, the sherds in this category are too small to determine whether the motif was curvilinear or rectilinear.

The most specific analytical groups are *curvilinear complicated stamped* and *rectilinear complicated stamped*. These groups include sherds featuring multiple parallel or intersecting curved lines in the case of the former and multiple intersecting straight lines in the latter case. In most cases, the small size of sherds makes identifying any particular motif very difficult. Motifs in the Townsend assemblage include concentric circles, concentric squares, figure nine and P scrolls, and wavy lines (Figure 4.7d). When a specific motif cannot be identified, the motif is recorded as "indeterminate." Sometimes, it is apparent that the motif is either a figure nine or a figure P, and in these cases the motif is recorded as "indeterminate scroll."

A number of other exterior surface treatments are also present in the Townsend pottery assemblage. Simple stamping is a rather difficult surface treatment to identify with certainty in samples dominated by small sherds. In keeping with the conservative structure of the hierarchical paddle-stamped classification method, I only identify sherds as simple stamped when two abutting edges of a single paddle are visible. Consequently, it is likely that the indeterminate linear-stamped category contains some simple-stamped sherds and that simple-stamped sherds are underrepresented in this analysis.

Cord marking, achieved by impressing the exterior surface of a wet vessel with a cord-wrapped paddle, is a rather common surface feature in the Townsend sample (Figure 4.7e). The size of the cordage wrapped around the paddle ranges from 1 to 6 mm, suggesting different types of materials were used. In virtually all cases in which the orientation of the sherd could be determined, the cord marking is arranged vertically. In one case, a cord-wrapped paddle was applied in such a way as to create a complex line block motif.

Scraped sherds feature prominent striations that are different from those present on sherds with plain surfaces. Rather than being caused by the dragging of temper particles across the surface of a vessel during smoothing, the striations present on scraped sherds were caused by a planar tool (probably made of shell or wood) that was used to thin the walls of a vessel. A small number of sherds exhibit surfaces that were battered or "roughened" with a corncob. This surface treatment is fairly easy to recognize even on small sherds given the distinct impressions left by the corn cupules.

Incised sherds feature straight or curved lines executed by dragging a pointed stylus across the exterior surface of a vessel. Most incised sherds in the Townsend sample are too small to identify a design motif; however, a few larger sherds bear recognizable motifs including line-filled triangles (Figure 4.7f), nested half squares, and parallel lines with semicircles.

Brushed surfaces evince a series of prominent striations that run in the same direction, usually perpendicular to the vessel lip. This surface treatment is distinguished from scraping by the depth of the striations and by the diagnostic ridges of clay that flank either side of each striation. These ridges represent the wake that results from dragging a bundle of twigs or some similar material across a wet vessel surface.

The remainder of the Townsend pottery sample is composed of exterior surface treatments that occur in very minor amounts. A few instances of body sherds bearing fingernail and stylus punctations are present, but the overwhelming majority of sherds bearing these modifications are rimstrips. The Townsend sample also includes two examples of large check stamping (>3 mm) and a single example of exterior red filming or slipping. Finally, the residual category *eroded* includes sherds with surfaces that have been severely worn to the point that any decorative surface treatment has been obliterated.

Ware Groups and Surface Treatments

Distinctions among the three potting traditions practiced by Townsend households are manifested in exterior surface treatments. These distinctions are readily apparent when the relative percentages of exterior surface treatments are compared across the three Cherokee pottery wares in the Townsend sample. The most striking distinction involves the predominance of plain surface treatments among the shell-tempered ware and the high frequencies of paddle-stamped surface treatments (i.e., indeterminate linear stamped, complicated stamped, curvilinear complicated stamped, simple stamped, and cord marked) among the gravel- and grit-tempered wares (Figure 4.8). Virtually all of the shell-tempered sherds evince plain, burnished, coarse plain, or scraped surfaces, compared to fewer than half of the gravel-tempered ware and a third of the grit-tempered ware. Conversely, fewer than 1 percent of shell-tempered sherds bear paddle-stamped surfaces, while these treatments make up over a third of the gravel-tempered assemblage and over half of the grit-tempered assemblage. Incising, while rare among gravel- and grit-tempered wares, is totally absent from the shell-tempered assemblage.

This major distinction involving plain and paddle-stamped surface treat-

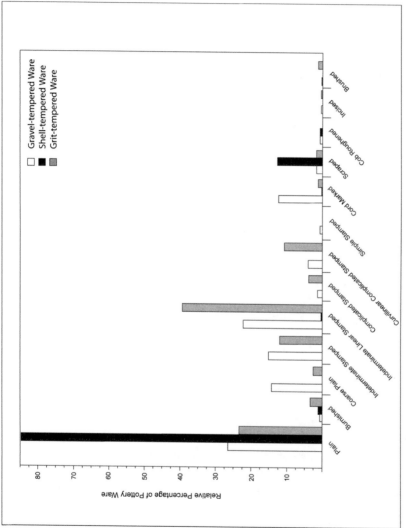

Figure 4.8. Relative percentages of exterior surface treatments among the three Cherokee temper groups at Townsend. This comparison only includes surface treatments comprising more than 1 percent of the total pottery sample recovered from Townsend.

ments sets the gravel-tempered and grit-tempered wares apart from the shell-tempered ware. A closer inspection of the relative frequencies of exterior surface treatments, however, reveals that the two rock-tempered wares also differ in a number of ways. First, while the collective proportion of plain, burnished, and coarse plain is roughly similar in gravel- and grit-tempered wares, coarse plain is a much more prevalent exterior surface treatment among gravel-tempered sherds (Figure 4.8). Second, indeterminate linear-stamped, complicated-stamped, and curvilinear complicated-stamped sherds are approximately twice as numerous in the grit-tempered assemblage as in the gravel-tempered assemblage. Third, although comprising only a small minority of the total sample, simple stamping only occurs on the gravel-tempered ware. Lastly, the proportion of cord marking in the gravel-tempered assemblage is significantly greater than that in the grit-tempered assemblage.

Vessel Form

Previous research has identified a number of different vessel forms associated with Overhill and Qualla series pottery assemblages (Bates 1986; Hally 1986b; King 1977; Riggs and Rodning 2002; Rodning 2004; Wilson and Rodning 2002). My definitions of vessel classes are informed by the functional analyses of historic and prehistoric Overhill, Qualla, and Lamar series vessels conducted by King (1977), Hally (1986a, 1986b), Wilson, and Rodning (Wilson and Rodning 2002). Collectively, these studies define a set of functional vessel classes based on shape, use wear, ethnohistoric accounts, and interviews with contemporary potters. In order to provide a relatively unbiased basis for quantitative comparison, the data are based on minimum number of vessels (MNV) estimates. MNV estimates have been derived using a number of methods, but I chose to base my MNV estimates solely on counts of unique rim sherds (Orton et al. 1993; Shapiro 1984; Wilson 2005). This method results in the most conservative vessel count estimates reflecting the composition of the vessel assemblages that were used and discarded by the Cherokee households at Townsend.

The Townsend pottery sample contains unique rim sherds representing a minimum of 329 vessels. These rim sherds can be sorted into four major vessel classes, including globular jars (n = 129), simple bowls (n = 13), restricted-orifice bowls (n = 34), and cazuelas (n = 17) (Figure 4.9; Table 4.2). The sample also includes a number of rimstrip fragments (n = 48) and rim sherds that were too small to confidently assign to a vessel class. With the exception of cazuelas, the relative frequencies of the three pottery wares among vessels are essentially the same as those of the body sherd sample.

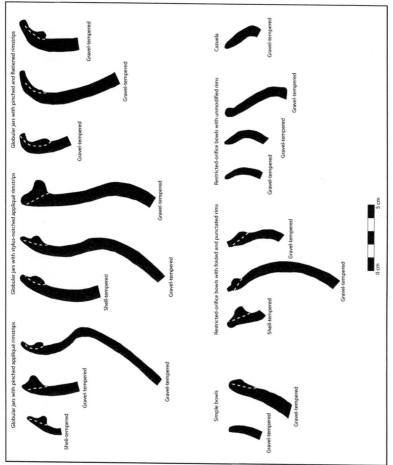

Figure 4.9. Profiles of vessel classes identified in the Townsend pottery assemblage.

Table 4.2. Minimum number of vessels (MNV) counts in the Townsend study sample

Basic Shape	n	%
Globular jar		
Gravel tempered	105	31.9
Shell tempered	14	4.3
Grit tempered	10	3.0
Total	129	39.2
Simple bowl		
Gravel tempered	11	3.3
Shell tempered	2	.7
Grit tempered	0	.0
Total	13	4.0
Restricted-orifice bowl		
Gravel tempered	30	9.1
Shell tempered	2	.6
Grit tempered	2	.6
Total	34	10.3
Cazuela		
Gravel tempered	16	4.9
Shell tempered	0	.0
Grit tempered	1	.3
Total	17	5.2
Indeterminate		
Gravel tempered	107	32.5
Shell tempered	17	5.2
Grit tempered	12	3.6
Total	136	41.3
Total	329	100.0

Globular Jars. The globular jar is by far the most common identifiable vessel class in the Townsend sample. This class includes vessels with re-curvate profiles featuring rounded bases, restricted necks, and excurvate to highly everted rims (Hally 1986b:277; King 1977:160; Shapiro 1984:702). The distribution of orifice diameter estimates suggests that jars were pro-duced in two sizes—small jars with orifice diameters ranging from 11 to 22 cm and large jars with orifice diameters ranging from 26 to 42 cm (Figure 4.10). The existence of two size classes among Townsend households is supported by the identification of an identical distribution of orifice di-ameters among the jar assemblage from the Coweeta Creek site (Wilson and Rodning 2002:30). Small jars in the Townsend sample are further dis-tinguished from large jars in that they possess unmodified rims (i.e., they lack rimstrips). Functional analyses and ethnohistoric accounts have dem-onstrated that large jars were most commonly used for preparing hominy, for cooking, and for storing large quantities of foodstuffs, while small jars were used to cook or reheat small quantities of food (Hally 1986b:269, 285–286; Wilson and Rodning 2002:31–32). King (1977:162–163) adds that the largest Cherokee jars could have acted as serving pots for large com-munal meals.

As with most Cherokee vessel assemblages, virtually all of the large jars in the Townsend sample possess thickened rims achieved by the addition of a rimstrip. In past work, the term *pinched rim jar* has been applied broadly to many large jars found in Cherokee assemblages (Hally 1986a; Wilson and Rodning 2002). This naming practice, however, is confusing, given that large jars in Cherokee assemblages typically exhibit a variety of different rimstrip elaborations, many of which are temporally diagnostic (e.g., Riggs and Rodning 2002; Rodning 2004; Shumate et al. 2005). Indeed, large jars in the Townsend sample can be divided into six groups based on distinct modes of rim elaboration (or lack thereof).

The three most common jar rim modes are excurvate rims with pinched appliqué rimstrips, excurvate rims with stylus-notched appliqué rimstrips, and highly everted rims with pinched and flattened rimstrips (Table 4.3; Figure 4.9). Because of their pronounced thickness, the first two rim modes are commonly referred to as *filleted* rimstrips, while the latter is the rim mode for which the term *pinched rim jar* was originally coined (Hally 1986b; Smith et al. 1988). Minority rim modes in the sample include 10 unmodi-fied rims, a single L-shaped rim, and three rolled rims. A jar rim sherd with a single lug handle and another exhibiting a strap handle are also present in the sample. Among the gravel-tempered and grit-tempered wares, jars with highly everted rims and pinched and flattened rimstrips by far outnumber jars with excurvate rims and pinched or notched appliqué rimstrips. Con-

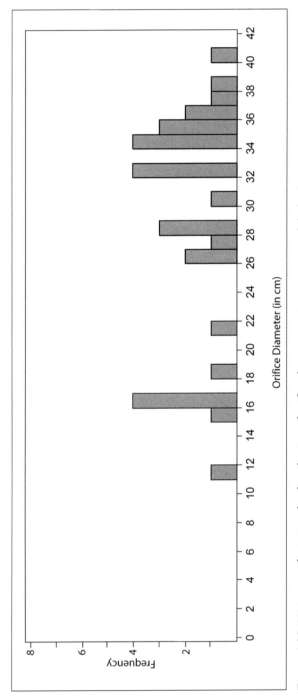

Figure 4.10. Histogram depicting the distribution of orifice diameter estimates among globular jars.

versely, in the shell-tempered ware group, jars with excurvate rims and pinched or notched appliqué rimstrips dominate, and jars with highly everted rims and pinched and flattened rimstrips are entirely absent.

Simple Bowls. This vessel class is characterized by a hemispherical profile featuring a rounded base. This class includes vessels whose orifice diameter is also the maximum diameter of the vessel. Both Hally (1986b:289) and King (1977:155) assign a serving function to simple bowls, pointing to the stability of this vessel form, the lack of evidence that it was used for cooking (i.e., exterior sooting and pitting), evidence of heavy use wear, and a large ratio of orifice diameter to depth.

Restricted-Orifice Bowls. Specimens belonging to this vessel class feature a hemispherical profile yet, as the name implies, they have inverted rather than vertical rims. Thus, unlike simple bowls, the maximum diameter of a restricted-orifice bowl is located beneath the lip—it is a shouldered vessel. Restricted-orifice bowls also differ in shape from cazuelas, another shouldered bowl form, in that they lack sharply carinated shoulders. In their analysis of the Coweeta Creek assemblage, Wilson and Rodning (2002:32) assign a serving function to restricted-orifice bowls on the basis of their size, lack of sooting, and shape. In regard to shape, they argue that the restricted orifice would have allowed for easier movement of food contents with a lower risk of spillage than a simple bowl form. The range of orifice diameters among restricted-orifice bowls in the Townsend sample (11–32 cm) is similar to that found by Wilson and Rodning (2002:32) for the same vessel class in the Coweeta Creek sample.

There are two major forms of restricted-orifice bowls in the Townsend assemblage—those with thickened rims and those with unmodified rims. The majority of restricted-orifice bowls possess thickened rims. The method used to thicken the rims of these bowls differs from that of jars in that most of the rims appear to have been folded rather than applied as a single coil. Consequently, rimstrips on restricted-orifice bowls tend to be narrower than those applied to globular jars. Furthermore, while pinching and stylus notching are present, stylus punctating and smoothing are the most common forms of rimstrip embellishment occurring on restricted-orifice bowls.

Cazuelas. Cazuelas, also known as carinated bowls, are vessels with inverted rims and sharply angled shoulders. Cazuelas possess either flat or round bases, although the latter form appears to be more common among historic-period Cherokee assemblages. None of the rim sherds in the Townsend sample is large enough to provide a reliable estimate of orifice diameter. Wilson and Rodning (2002:33) report a size range of 9 to 30 cm for cazuelas in the Coweeta Creek sample, and it is likely that the Townsend cazuelas

Table 4.3. Exterior surface treatments and rim modes applied to large globular jars in the Townsend sample

	Plain	Burnished	Coarse Plain	Indeterminate Stamped	Indeterminate Linear Stamped	Curvilinear Complicated Stamped	Cord Marked	Scraped	Eroded	Total
Gravel-tempered jars										
Excurvate rims with pinched appliqué rimstrips	18	0	4	0	1	0	0	0	0	23
Excurvate rims with notched appliqué rimstrips	5	0	6	1	0	0	3	1	0	16
Highly everted rims with pinched and flattened rimstrips	35	1	5	3	5	1	1	0	0	51
L-shaped rims	0	0	0	0	0	0	0	0	0	0
Rolled rims	1	1	0	0	0	0	0	0	0	2
Unmodified rims	5	0	0	0	1	0	1	1	0	8
Shell-tempered jars										
Excurvate rims with pinched appliqué rimstrips	5	0	0	0	0	0	0	0	1	6

										Total
Excurvate rims with notched appliqué rimstrips	5	0	0	0	0	0	0	0	1	6
Highly everted rims with pinched and flattened rimstrips	0	0	0	0	0	0	0	0	0	0
L-shaped rims	0	0	0	0	0	0	0	0	0	0
Rolled rims	1	0	0	0	0	0	0	0	0	1
Unmodified rims	0	0	0	0	0	0	0	0	0	0
Grit-tempered jars										
Excurvate rims with pinched appliqué rimstrips	2	0	0	0	0	0	0	0	0	2
Excurvate rims with notched appliqué rimstrips	1	0	0	0	0	0	0	0	0	1
Highly everted rims with pinched and flattened rimstrips	4	0	0	0	0	0	0	0	0	4
L-shaped rims	0	0	0	0	0	0	0	0	0	0
Rolled rims	1	0	0	0	0	0	0	0	0	1
Unmodified rims	1	0	0	0	0	0	0	0	1	2
Total	84	2	15	4	8	1	5	2	2	123

are similar in size to the other bowl forms. Shape, evidence of use wear, and the common presence of exterior sooting have led researchers to conclude that cazuelas were multipurpose vessels used in food preparation, cooking, and serving (Hally 1986b:288–289; King 1977:159; Shapiro 1984:707; Wilson and Rodning 2002:33). Aside from their distinctive shape, cazuelas typically lack rim modification and evince incised decoration above the vessel shoulder (Shumate et al. 2005:6.11; Wilson and Rodning 2002:33). All but two of the cazuelas in the Townsend sample bear incised decorations between the vessel shoulder and lip. Four of the specimens are decorated with line-filled triangle motifs, and single specimens bear nested half squares and lines and semicircles motifs. Sixteen of the cazuelas in the Townsend sample are gravel tempered and one is grit tempered. The cazuela form is not represented among the shell-tempered ware.

VARIABILITY AMONG TOWNSEND HOUSEHOLD POTTERY ASSEMBLAGES

Thus far, I have identified a number of significant differences within the Townsend pottery assemblage in the dimensions of pottery ware, exterior surface treatment, and vessel form. Differences in four paste attributes (temper material, temper particle size, density of temper particles, and vessel wall thickness) indicate that the Cherokee households at Townsend were making pottery vessels in three different wares, each of which was intentionally created through the manipulation of paste composition. Distinctions were also expressed as differences in surface treatment and vessel form. Virtually all of the shell-tempered ware was plain, while the majority of both gravel-tempered and grit-tempered wares were paddle stamped. These latter two wares could also be distinguished by the popularity of plain and cord-marked sherds among the gravel-tempered ware and the relatively high proportions of linear-stamped and complicated-stamped sherds among the grit-tempered ware. Whereas the various vessel forms composing the gravel-tempered and grit-tempered MNV assemblages were present in roughly similar proportions, jars with highly everted rims and pinched and flattened rimstrips and cazuelas were completely absent from the shell-tempered MNV assemblage.

The last piece of evidence I marshal in support of my argument involves the spatial distribution of these potting styles among Townsend households. Are the three potting styles present in each of the Townsend household pottery assemblages in equal proportions? If not, how do differences in the relative composition of household pottery assemblages spatially map onto the community? I answer these questions by conducting a correspondence analysis (CA) of household pottery assemblages in order to identify consistent associations of ware groups and exterior surface treatments among household assemblages (see Appendix A for an explanation of this exploratory data analysis technique). One of the most useful results of CA is a biplot that depicts the relative degree of association of household pottery assemblages, as well as that of the different combinations of pottery ware and exterior surface treatment. In interpreting the biplot, one can infer that the pottery types located near one another in the biplot typically occur together in the same contexts, that household assemblages located near one another have similar pottery assemblages, and that the pottery types located near each household assemblage in the biplot represent the dominant types in each of those assemblages. The distribution presented in the biplot accounts for 85.9 percent of the variability in the data matrix.

The biplot resulting from this CA not only reveals the previously identified pattern in the distribution of the three pottery wares but also identifies significant patterning in the household-level distributions of surface treatments (Figure 4.11). Clustering of the locations of the household-level pottery assemblages in the biplot (indicated by open diamond symbols) suggests that the assemblages associated with Household 1 and Household 2 are similar and those associated with Household 4, Household 5, and Household 6 are similar. Furthermore, the locations of these clusters at opposite ends of the x-axis indicate a large degree of difference between these pottery assemblages. The assemblage associated with Household 3 is different from both of these clusters. Considering the distributions of the pottery types, it is clear that the assemblages associated with Household 1 and Household 2 are dominated by shell tempering and plain, burnished, and scraped exterior surface treatments. The assemblages associated with Households 4, 5, and 6 are significantly different, being made up primarily of gravel-tempered and grit-tempered paddle-stamped wares. The pottery assemblage associated with Household 3 differs from the other two clusters in its lack of shell-tempered ware and the predominance of plain, coarse plain, and burnished surface treatments. Also, the distribution of these three different pottery assemblage clusters is replicated in the actual spatial distribution of the Townsend households. Shell-tempered plain wares are concentrated in the two westernmost households while the pottery assemblages associated with the eastern households are dominated by gravel-tempered and grit-tempered paddle-stamped pottery (see also Howell 2005).

The relative proportions of different functional classes among household vessel assemblages are surprisingly similar considering the great variability in pottery ware and external surface treatments. Ignoring differences in rim modes among globular jars, the vessel assemblages (measured using MNV) associated with Households 1, 2, 3, and 4 contain very similar proportions of globular jars, restricted-orifice bowls, and simple bowls (Table 4.4; Figure 4.12). The vessel assemblages associated with Households 5

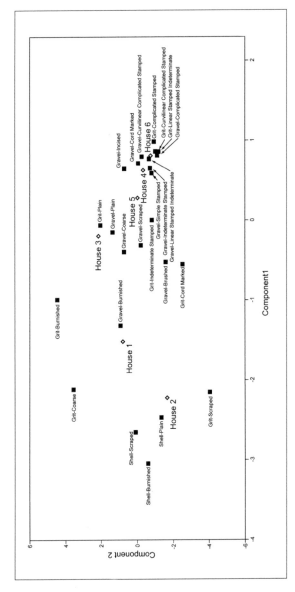

Figure 4.11. Biplot depicting the results of the correspondence analysis conducted on household pottery assemblages at Townsend.

Table 4.4. Composition of household vessel assemblages (measured in MNV) at Townsend

Household	Large Jars w/ Pinched Appliqué Rimstrips		Large Jars w/ Notched Appliqué Rimstrips		Large Jars w/ Pinched and Flattened Rimstrips		Other Large Jars		Restricted-Orifice Bowls		Simple Bowls		Cazuelas		Total	
	n	%	n	%	n	%	n	%	n	%	n	%	n	%	n	%
1	4	17	10	44	0	0	2	4	6	26	2	9	0	0	24	100
2	4	20	8	40	1	5	0	0	6	30	1	5	0	0	20	100
3	3	25	3	25	1	8	3	25	1	8	1	8	0	0	12	100
4	19	17	1	<1	48	43	6	5	18	16	6	5	8	7	106	95[a]

[a]This total is less than 100 percent because the Household 4 vessel assemblage also includes six small jars, a vessel class that was not present in any other household context and thus was not included in this tally.

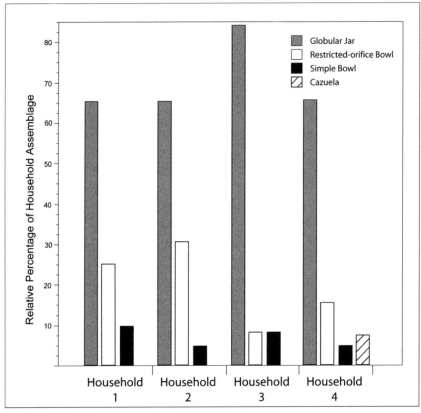

Figure 4.12. Comparison of vessel assemblages among Townsend households.

and 6 are not included in this comparison because the former assemblage is dominated by sherds from a single pit feature and the latter assemblage only contains two unique vessel rims.

REGIONAL ASSOCIATIONS OF THE TOWNSEND POTTING TRADITIONS

Are there ties between the three potting traditions practiced by Townsend households and those identified at other Cherokee sites? How does the pottery assemblage from Townsend compare with "classic" Overhill and Qualla series assemblages? In order to answer these questions and better characterize the variability in the Townsend pottery sample within the larger geographic and temporal context of the English Contact period, I make comparisons with pottery samples from a number of Cherokee contexts at other sites including the Ocoee site, the Chota-Tanasee site (Bates 1986), the Tomotley site (Baden 1983), the Mialoquo site (Russ and Chapman 1983), the Tuckaseegee site (Keel 1976), the Coweeta Creek site (Rodning 2004), the Alarka farmstead site (Shumate et al. 2005), and the Chattooga site.

Comparisons with Overhill Series Pottery Samples

I could not identify a comparable data set derived from a reliably dated English Contact period Overhill context. The closest candidate is the Ocoee site, located at the juncture of the Ocoee and Hiwassee rivers far to the south of the Townsend site (Lewis et al. 1995:562–588). This location and diagnostic European artifacts recovered from the site suggest a correspondence with the late seventeenth- and early eighteenth-century Overhill Cherokee town of Amoyee. Based on the frequency data presented by Lewis et al. (1995:Table 30.4), it appears that the Ocoee pottery sample was dominated by shell-tempered plain ware. Only two shell-tempered complicated-stamped sherds were noted, along with 30 "rock-tempered" complicated-stamped sherds. My inspection of the surviving pottery collection from the site corroborates these proportions, although I was only able to locate rim sherds and a small portion of the body sherd sample. I recorded 34 rim sherds, 33 of which were shell tempered and one of which was gravel tempered like those from Townsend. I also identified four body sherds in the type collection that were grit tempered and fit the description of Qualla series pottery. Thirty-one of the shell-tempered sherds had plain surfaces and two were incised (one with a lines-and-semicircles motif and one bearing parallel diagonal lines); the gravel-tempered sherd was plain; and the four grit-tempered sherds were curvilinear complicated stamped with indeterminate motifs. In regard to vessel forms, the Ocoee sample included 21 shell-tempered globular jars, 3 with pinched appliqué rimstrips and 18 with notched appliqué rimstrips; a single gravel-tempered globular jar with a notched appliqué rimstrip; two shell-tempered simple bowls, both with notched appliqué rimstrips; and three shell-tempered restricted-orifice bowls, one with a folded and punctated rim and one with a folded and notched rim.

A thumbnail-sketch comparison of this sample with the Townsend sample reveals that (1) the Ocoee site sample contains a much higher proportion of shell-tempered sherds than the Townsend sample; (2) the Ocoee sample has a much higher proportion of plain ware than the Townsend sample; (3) Ocoee vessel forms are by and large very similar to those found at Townsend; and (4) the absence of two vessel classes in the Ocoee sample (i.e., globular jars with highly everted rims and pinched and flattened rimstrips and cazuelas) is interesting in that these same vessel forms are missing in the shell-tempered ware found at Townsend. Although highly speculative, these patterns suggest that the potters of at least one Cherokee community were practicing a potting tradition centered around shell-tempered plain ware during the late seventeenth and early eighteenth centuries. Indulging the urge to push this tenuous interpretation further, this potting tradition appears to be related to the one practiced by some of the potters living at Townsend (i.e., Households 1 and 2).

With the exception of the Ocoee sample, all of the well-documented Overhill Cherokee pottery collections recovered from professional excavations date to between the mid-eighteenth and early nineteenth centuries—at least 50 years later than the estimated Cherokee occupation at Townsend. While these collections do little to improve our understanding of Cherokee potting traditions during the English Contact period, they are nevertheless important because they provide a diachronic dimension to the study of Overhill Cherokee pottery. Comparing these collections to the Townsend sample, one can identify changes that occurred in Overhill Cherokee potting practices between the time when Townsend was occupied and later in the eighteenth century. This comparison utilizes published data associated with excavations at the Chota-Tanasee site (Bates 1986:289–305), the Tomotley site (Baden 1983:37–62), and the Mialoquo site (Russ and Chapman 1983:69–83). I found that while the abundance of plain-surfaced pottery in the Townsend sample is similar to that found in later Overhill contexts, the predominance of rock-tempered wares and much higher frequencies of cord marking and paddle-stamped surface treatments in the Townsend sample are strikingly different from the much more homogenous Overhill samples (Marcoux 2008:Table 6.13).

Comparisons with Qualla Series Pottery Samples

The differences that set the Townsend pottery sample apart from those associated with other sites producing Overhill Cherokee pottery beg for comparisons to pottery samples recovered from Cherokee sites located farther afield. Pottery samples used in this comparison were recovered from the following contexts: (1) a trash deposit located between the floor and the collapsed walls of a catastrophically burned winter house at the Tuckaseegee site (Keel 1976); (2) a large refuse-filled pit (Feature 72) at the Coweeta Creek site (Rodning 2004); (3) all of the archaeological features and excavation units associated with the Alarka farmstead (Shumate et al. 2005); and (4) a trash deposit located around the central hearth of a winter house at the Chattooga site. These contexts were chosen for quantitative comparison with the household pottery assemblages at Townsend because the samples drawn from them represent the pottery use and discard practices of single households over relatively brief periods of time (certainly less than a decade) during the English Contact period. This set of comparisons is in the same vein as those presented above and focuses primarily on pottery ware, surface treatment, and vessel form.

One sees a similar pattern of contrast to that seen in the comparison of pottery samples from Townsend and Ocoee. There is a sharp contrast between the diversity of pottery wares found in Townsend household assemblages, on the one hand, and the single grit-tempered pottery ware present in the assemblages from the other sites. Indeed, with the exception of a single shell-tempered body sherd from the Alarka site (Shumate et al. 2005:6.4), the pottery ware of all potsherds in the comparative assemblages conforms to the definition of the Qualla series (Egloff 1967; Keel 1976; Riggs and Rodning 2002; Rodning 2004; Ward and Davis 1999; Wilson and Rodning 2002; see also Marcoux 2008:Table 6.14).

Clear patterning emerges when variability in relative frequencies of surface treatments is considered—patterning that reflects both regional and temporal differences among the samples. As in the household-level analysis of Townsend pottery samples, the comparison of frequency data is greatly aided by CA. The results of the CA, depicted graphically as a biplot (Figure 4.13), indicate that the pottery samples are distributed in four discrete clusters. One cluster, which includes the samples from Townsend Households 1, 2, and 3, is dominated by plain and coarse plain surface treatments. The second cluster, containing pottery samples from Townsend Households 4, 5, and 6, is defined by lesser amounts of plain and coarse plain sherds and greater numbers of cord-marked and paddle-stamped sherds. The third cluster includes the samples from the Tuckaseegee and Alarka sites. The samples in this cluster are dominated by curvilinear complicated-stamped pottery and contain very little plain or coarse plain ware. The fourth cluster includes pottery samples from the Coweeta Creek and Chattooga sites. These samples include plain, coarse plain, and indeterminate linear-stamped sherds in similar proportions to the Tuckaseegee and Alarka samples; however, rectilinear complicated-stamped sherds comprise a much higher percentage of the Coweeta Creek and Chattooga samples.

Given that distance in the CA biplot can be thought of as a measure of similarity among the samples, two conclusions can be drawn. First, the pottery samples from Townsend demonstrate a significant amount of interhousehold variability with regard to surface treatment; however, when compared with "classic" Qualla series samples from Cherokee sites in other settlement divisions, the Townsend household assemblages form a geographically distinct potting tradition typified by plain, coarse plain, and cord-

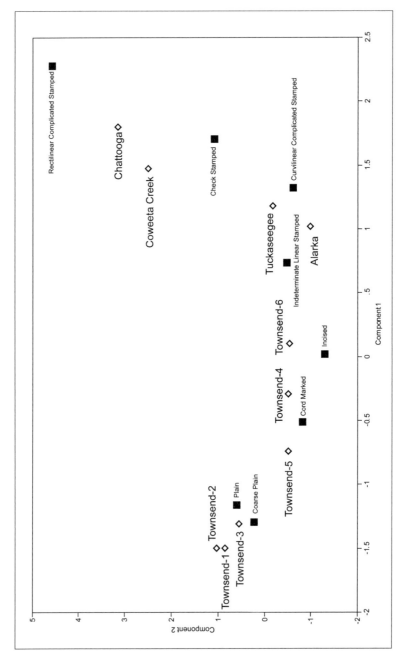

Figure 4.13. Biplot depicting the results of the correspondence analysis conducted on pottery assemblages from the six Townsend households and other selected Cherokee sites.

marked surface treatments. Second, the samples that are most similar to the Townsend households are those recovered from the Tuckaseegee and Alarka sites. Conversely, the composition of the pottery samples from the Coweeta Creek and Chattooga sites differs dramatically from that of the Townsend household samples with regard to surface treatment. According to the current ceramic chronology for Qualla series pottery, the Tuckaseegee and Alarka assemblages clearly date to the late Middle Qualla phase while those of the Coweeta Creek and Chattooga sites are associated with the early Late Qualla phase (Riggs and Rodning 2002; Rodning 2004; Shumate et al. 2005). The CA thus strongly suggests that the Cherokee household occupations at Townsend all date to the period from 1650 to 1720. The temporal placement of the Townsend household occupations in this period finds corroboration in the other dating measures including archaeomagnetism and glass bead chronology (Lengyel 2004; Marcoux 2008).

SUMMARY AND DISCUSSION

At the close of this chapter, I wish to emphasize five main conclusions drawn from my analyses and comparisons. First, quantitative analysis clearly suggests that there were three distinct potting traditions practiced by Townsend potters. These traditions were based on three different pottery wares and involved significant differences in surface treatment and to a lesser extent vessel form.

Second, while not mutually exclusive, the spatial distributions of pottery wares and surface treatments strongly suggest that particular potting traditions were associated with particular households. The pottery samples recovered from Households 1 and 2, for example, were overwhelmingly dominated by the shell-tempered plain pottery associated with the Overhill ceramic series. Samples from Households 3, 4, and 5, in contrast, contained large amounts of gravel-tempered plain-surfaced and paddle-stamped pottery. I refer to this heretofore undefined local Cherokee potting tradition as the *Tuckaleechee series*. While the sample from Household 6 was not very large, it did contain an unusual abundance of grit-tempered curvilinear complicated-stamped pottery, a hallmark of the Qualla ceramic series.

Third, the pottery assemblages recovered from Townsend households are very different from existing Overhill Cherokee pottery assemblages. Whereas Townsend pottery is defined by diversity in paste and surface treatment, assemblages from the late seventeenth-century Overhill site of Ocoee and later eighteenth-century Overhill sites are largely homogenous and consist of shell-tempered vessels with plain surfaces. Considering the predominance of rock tempering and paddle stamping in the Townsend assemblage, one must conclude that these assemblages are more similar to contemporaneous Qualla series assemblages even though the Townsend site is located within what is historically thought of as Overhill Cherokee territory.

Fourth, when exterior surface treatment and vessel form are compared with those of English Contact period Cherokee assemblages from other sites, Townsend households form a distinct cluster. Furthermore, Townsend pottery assemblages are more closely related to late seventeenth-century Qualla assemblages (i.e., Alarka and Tuckaseegee) than to early eighteenth-century Qualla assemblages (Coweeta Creek and Chattooga).

Fifth, the ceramic diversity found in the Townsend pottery sample is not without precedent in Cherokee archaeology. Indeed, a similar degree of ceramic diversity is present in the pottery samples from the late eighteenth-century sites of Tomotley and Mialoquo, Cherokee settlements that were composed of both local Overhill groups and refugee populations fleeing the Cherokee Lower Towns during the Revolutionary War. Drawing an analogy to these sites, I offer this conclusion—that the distinct potting traditions practiced by the Townsend households represent a similar social situation to that which occurred at Tomotley and Mialoquo. In this case, however, the Townsend community was an amalgam of households from different Cherokee settlements that, like many other Indian groups across the Southeast, formed a coalescent community as a strategy to negotiate the population loss and violence associated with the shatter zone between 1670 and 1715 (Hudson 2002; Kowalewski 2006).

As defined in Hudson (2002) and Kowalewski (2006) and in other works, coalescent societies were formed by remnant or refugee groups as a strategic response to demographic collapse and other pressures associated with the southeastern shatter zone. Examples of coalescent societies dating to the English Contact period include the Creek (Knight 1994), the Choctaw (Galloway 1995), the Catawba (Merrell 1989a), and Piedmont North Carolina groups (Davis 2002). Kowalewski (2006) argues that coalescence is not a societal type but a strategy that plays out in very different ways depending upon local historical contingencies (Kowalewski 2006:120–121).

In the case of Townsend, I believe that the households were pursuing a strategy of coalescence. These folk came together from different Cherokee communities to settle in a previously unoccupied area amidst the turmoil of the shatter zone. The choices that Townsend potters made with respect to tempering material, external surface treatment, and vessel form were all informed by different "constellations of knowledge" or notions about the proper way that things are done (Sinclair 2000). These constellations of knowledge were passed on generationally through the repetitious act of making pots and teaching others to make pots. At the risk of partaking in the arcane cultural arithmetic of "pottery equals people," I believe that the results of the pottery analyses suggest some possibilities for where the Townsend potters could have originated. The potting traditions associated with the Overhill series and Qualla series do have defined geographical distributions. Overhill series pottery has a local (i.e., eastern Tennessee) antecedent in the pottery of the Dallas phase, although a direct temporal link between these phases has yet to be established (Schroedl 1986). Qualla pottery has a much better-defined geographic distribution centered in the Cherokee Lower, Middle, and Out towns. The third and most common potting tradition represented in Townsend household assemblages has no known antecedent and combines aspects of both Overhill and Qualla series. More research is needed, but at this point I will speculate that either this tradition was rooted in a potting tradition that existed formerly elsewhere (perhaps in the Nolichucky River valley) or it was a novel tradition that developed locally out of the negotiation of daily life by potters who lived together and shared their distinct constellations of knowledge.

5

Space and Time in the Daily Lives of Townsend Households

Landscapes like the one occupied by the Cherokee households in Tucka-leechee Cove are materializations of a diachronic relationship between people and space, particularly the ways in which spaces are made "social places" through daily practices and, conversely, the ways that these places influence practice (e.g., Allen et al. 1998; Appadurai 1997; Lefebvre 1991; Low and Zúñiga 2003). This dialectical relationship between space, time, and daily life plays out on various scales from the region down to the individual household. In this chapter, I consult architectural and subsurface pit feature data in order to explore how domestic space and time both reflected and structured the daily practices of Cherokee households in the Townsend community. I begin with a brief review of eighteenth- and nineteenth-century Cherokee architecture based on ethnohistoric accounts. I then describe the architectural characteristics of the structures found at the Townsend site, focusing on method of manufacture, household size, and occupation duration.

Comparing data from the Townsend structures with those from various protohistoric and historic Cherokee sites in eastern Tennessee and western North Carolina, I find that in adapting to the pervasive demographic and economic disruptions wrought during this period, Cherokee households, including those at the Townsend site, enacted a number of strategic changes in their daily lives. Significant among these were changes that resulted in fundamental alterations in community spatial organization, the methods used to manufacture and repair houses, and the occupation duration of particular domestic spaces—namely, households became more dispersed within towns, houses were built much less robustly, houses were repaired in a piecemeal rather than an *en toto* fashion, and the tenure of households within a given domestic space was dramatically shortened. Unlike in earlier times, household identities in English Contact period Cherokee communities do not appear to have involved strong historical ties with a particular place on the landscape. Given the frequent intrusion of disease and violence into Indian communities at this time, I conclude that the untethering of Cherokee households from the landscape constituted a strategic response to the increasing uncertainty of the period.

ETHNOHISTORIC DESCRIPTIONS OF EIGHTEENTH- AND EARLY NINETEENTH-CENTURY CHEROKEE ARCHITECTURE

Reconstructing the forms, functions, and use histories of structures from the dregs of archaeological data is one of the more difficult tasks archaeologists face (e.g., Blanton 1994; Wilk and Rathje 1982). In undertaking this task, archaeologists studying eighteenth- and early nineteenth-century Cherokee architecture are extremely fortunate to be able to reference a rich body of period descriptions (for a list of these see Schroedl, ed. 1986; see also Adair 1986 [1775]; Bartram 1996 [1791]; Norton 1970 [1816]; and Timberlake 2001 [1762]). In the interest of space and in order to avoid duplicating the diligent work of others, here I will limit my discussion to the major themes of these descriptions. For further study, the reader is encouraged to seek out the original accounts or consult the thorough synthesis provided by Schroedl (ed. 1986:217–228).

Virtually all of the historic descriptions of Cherokee structures are couched in terms of a public/domestic architectural vernacular expressed as the opposition between large townhouse structures and smaller household dwellings. Descriptions of so-called winter townhouses or rotundas from the mid-eighteenth and early nineteenth centuries, most notably those of Adair (1986 [1775]:453), Bartram (1996 [1791]:299–300), Norton (1970 [1816]:54), and Timberlake (2001 [1762]:59), agree that these were very large round or polygonal wooden structures that could house several hundred people. One of the main features of these substantially built structures was the central roof supports—massive wooden posts, 3–4 m in length, which formed a square or ring at the center of the townhouse. The outer walls of the townhouse were constructed of interwoven cane or bark mats secured to upright posts and covered in clay daub. The roof was covered in bark and a layer of soil. Entrance to the building was gained through a very small doorway, which opened into an expansive inner chamber lined with benches for sitting. At the center of the townhouse was a formal hearth, where a fire was kept alight constantly. Period descriptions sometimes mentioned a companion structure, known as a summer townhouse, ramada, or pavilion. These appear to have been much less formal structures with rectangular floor plans and open sides. These buildings were used for community rituals and meetings during warmer months.

Of greater import to the study of the structures at the Townsend site are extant eighteenth- and nineteenth-century descriptions of Cherokee domestic dwellings. These descriptions highlight the fact that, like townhouse architecture, Cherokee domestic architecture was manifest in a seasonal dichotomy of paired winter and summer structures (Adair 1986 [1775]:448–450; Bartram 1996 [1791]:298–299; Norton 1970 [1816]:141; Timberlake 2001 [1762]:84). Winter domestic structures, sometimes called hot houses or *asi*, were essentially smaller versions of winter townhouses built using the same architectural principles. The framework of these round or octagonal structures consisted of four large central roof support posts arranged in a square surrounded by an outer ring of upright posts, which formed the outer walls. Like townhouses, the walls of winter houses were described as being daubed and the roof was covered in a layer of soil. Also like the townhouses, these structures had a single small doorway, benches lining the walls, and a central hearth. Summer houses were described as smaller analogs to the townhouse ramada or pavilion. They were lightly built rectangular structures located within a few meters of the winter house. Summer houses contained a hearth and interior benches, they were sometimes divided into three compartments, and they sometimes featured one open side.

According to some historic accounts, the use of paired seasonal domestic structures was a widespread and long-lived practice among southeastern Indian communities. Adair (1986 [1775]:448–450), for example, wrote that dual house forms were embraced by many southeastern Indian groups in the late eighteenth century, and Norton's journal (1970 [1816]:141) stated that some folk in Cherokee and Creek communities still used winter houses as late as 1810. At this time, however, Norton also observed that many Cherokee were abandoning the use of paired winter–summer houses in favor of European style log cabins.

Cherokee Architecture at the Townsend Site

Over the past few decades, there have been a number of archaeological projects that have included the excavation and analysis of prehistoric and historic Cherokee structures (e.g., Baden 1983; Cable and Reed 2000; Chapman 1979; Coe 1961; Dickens 1976, 1979; Guthe and Bistline 1981; Keel

1976; Marcoux 2008; Polhemus 1987; Riggs 1989; Rodning 2002, 2004; Russ and Chapman 1983; Schroedl 1989; Schroedl, ed. 1986). These works have provided the foundations for developing a diachronic perspective on Cherokee architecture that allows researchers to explore relationships among architectural forms that existed before and after European contact (*sensu* Hally 2002). How does the architecture uncovered at the Townsend site fit into this picture?

Ten definitive Cherokee structures and associated Cherokee pit features are widely distributed across the Townsend site in six discrete clusters, each representing a single household (Figure 3.6). Two of these households consist of paired winter and summer dwellings; one household consists of a winter dwelling, a summer dwelling, and a ramada; and two households consist of single winter houses (Figure 5.1). The architectural form of the final household (Structure 27) could not be determined as confidently because the structures were not identified in the field and the postholes composing the structures were not excavated.

Assessing the Method of Manufacture of Cherokee Structures at Townsend

While archaeological excavations have confirmed the ethnohistoric descriptions of house construction on a general level, analyses of architectural data typically lack the kind of empirical specificity that allows for more objective intrasite and intersite comparisons of Cherokee house construction methods. In this section I offer one way to better link our interpretations of Cherokee architecture to archaeological data. Specifically, I believe that the ethnohistoric descriptions provide three important expectations regarding the archaeological manifestation of Cherokee structures as posthole patterns: (1) there should be different types of postholes creating the posthole patterns of summer houses and winter houses—deep, large-diameter postholes that were dug to accept central roof supports, and smaller diameter perimeter postholes that were dug for posts that supported wall plates; (2) in winter houses, the large deeply dug postholes representing the central roof supports should form a quadrangle in the center of a round or octagonal pattern of postholes representing the structure walls; and (3) in a summer house, the large deeply dug postholes representing the central roof supports should be arranged in a line down the center of a rectangular arrangement of postholes representing the structure walls. The first expectation, that there will be multiple types of posts, should be evident as multiple modes in the distribution of posthole depths, as well as significant

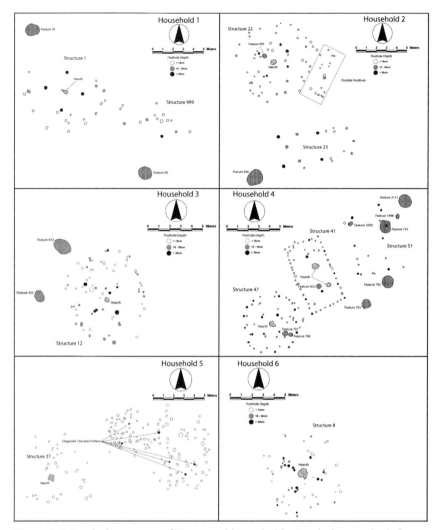

Figure 5.1. Posthole patterns of Townsend households. Postholes are shaded to indicate depth.

differences in the median depths and/or diameters among posthole types. The second and third expectations regarding the arrangement of different post types in winter and summer houses can be tested by exploring the spatial distribution of posthole types on plan view drawings of the structures. For the most part, the expectations are borne out by the architectural data recorded for the Cherokee structures at the Townsend site (see also Shumate et al. 2005).

Testing the first expectation, the sample for the analyses consists of all excavated postholes associated with Cherokee structures at the Townsend site with the exception of one structure in which the postholes were not excavated. The distribution of posthole depths does indeed suggest the existence of separate types of postholes (Figure 5.2). Inspection of Figure 5.2 reveals a trimodal distribution of posthole depths, with modes at 11 cm, 21 cm, and 38 cm. Three post types are defined by these modes: one type includes postholes less than 15 cm deep, one type includes postholes 16–30 cm deep, and one type includes posts greater than 30 cm deep. Further distinctions in posthole types can be made when the locations of the postholes are considered along with depth (Figure 5.3). Postholes greater than 30 cm deep located in the center of structures represent central roof supports. Postholes less than 30 cm deep located more than 50 cm inside of the outer perimeter postholes are deemed interior posts. Postholes greater than 15 cm deep comprising the outer perimeter of a structure are considered exterior support posts, while those perimeter postholes less than 15 cm deep are simply called exterior posts.

When the postholes are shaded to represent the three depth classes, their distribution in plan view structure drawings demonstrates patterning consistent with the second and third expectations mentioned above. All of the round structures, which presumably represent winter houses, contain at least one set of four central postholes greater than 30 cm deep and arranged in a quadrangle (Figure 5.1). These structures are also defined by a circular, relatively evenly spaced pattern of postholes with a floor area of approximately 40 m^2 (Table 5.1). In two cases (Structure 22 and Structure 47), the posthole patterns of the perimeter walls feature widely spaced deep postholes interspersed with shallow postholes. In these structures, the deeper postholes may correspond to corner posts that linked the wall segments of the winter houses. This posthole pattern has been identified in the winter houses at the Chota-Tanasee site and at the Alarka site (Schroedl, ed. 1986:267; Shumate et al. 2005:5.26–5.27). The exterior wall support posts of two other Townsend winter houses (Structure 12 and Structure 8) are more widely spaced and are clustered in sets of two and three. Interior posts, those less than 30 cm deep and located more than 50 cm inside the structure walls, appear to have filled two functions. Some of these posts cluster near the central roof support posts and likely acted as additional roof braces. The other interior posts either supported sleeping benches, as described in ethnohistoric accounts, or formed interior partitions within the structure.

Of the structures that may be considered summer houses, only Structure 41 has a posthole pattern consistent with the expectations generated by Adair's description. This house, which has two large-diameter, deep post-

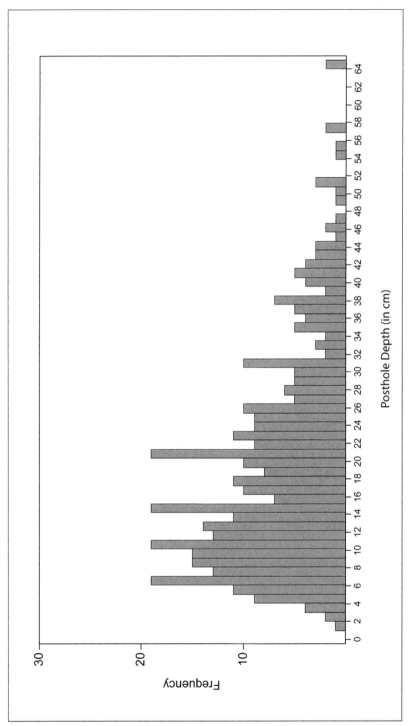

Figure 5.2. Histogram depicting the distribution of posthole depths for Cherokee structures at Townsend.

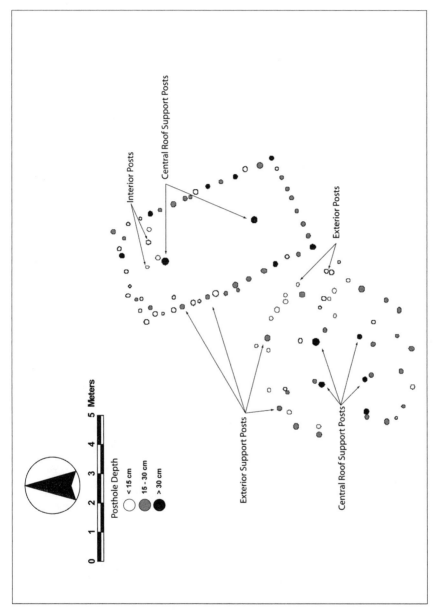

Figure 5.3. Hypothetical examples of post types based on posthole depth and location within structures.

Table 5.1. Architectural data for Townsend structures

Structure	Shape	Structure Type	Orientation[a]	Major Axis (m)	Minor Axis (m)	Area (m²)	Total Posts	Post Spacing (m)[b]	Estimated Household Size (in persons)
1	Circular	Winter house	Cardinal	8.05	7.50	44.31	22	1.85	7
8	Octagonal	Winter house	Intercardinal	7.50	6.70	38.08	56	.97	6
12	Circular	Winter house	Intercardinal	8.10	7.00	44.29	75	.68	7
22	Octagonal w/ vestibule	Winter house	Intercardinal	8.20	7.50	45.31	58	.85	8
23	Rectangular	Summer house	E–W	7.40	3.25	22.64	18	1.20	
27	Undetermined	Winter house?	n/a	n/a	n/a	n/a	32	n/a	n/a
41	Rectangular	Summer house	NW–SE	7.85	4.28	30.75	58	.50	
47	Octagonal	Winter house	Intercardinal	7.70	6.70	36.70	52	.77	6
51	Rectangular	Summer house	NW–SE	7.60	4.50	28.81	18	1.37	
999	Rectangular?	Summer house?	E–W	7.00	4.00	22.90	15	n/a	

[a]Orientation was determined by the major axis of rectangular structures and by the locations of the four main roof supports for circular or octagonal structures.
[b]Circumference in meters divided by number of posts.

holes located down the centerline of the structure, is similar in form to the summer house identified by Shumate (Shumate et al. 2005) at the Alarka site (Figure 5.1). The other structures in this group lack central roof support posts and thus could not have supported ridgepoles or peaked gabled roofs. Lacking central support posts, these structures would have instead had single-faced slanted roofs supported by the exterior wall posts. The posthole patterns of Structure 51 and Structure 23, which are made up almost entirely of postholes over 15 cm in depth, support this interpretation. These structures are similar in form to the summer houses identified by Schroedl (ed. 1986) at Chota-Tanasee. Interior postholes are for the most part lacking in the Townsend summer houses with the exception of Structure 41, which has a series of posts (perhaps forming an entrance baffle) in its northeast corner.

Assessing Household Size from Cherokee Structures at Townsend

Working from historical data and interviews with Cherokee informants, twentieth-century ethnologists clearly identified the household as the fundamental social unit in Cherokee communities stretching back at least to the eighteenth century (Gearing 1962:18–20; Gilbert 1943:202–203). These households were largely based on coresidence and were formed around the nuclear family (i.e., husband, wife, and children), but they could also include members of the extended family. What was the demographic makeup of the households who built and dwelt in the structures excavated at Townsend? Unfortunately, there is no way to reconstruct the specific demographic makeup of each household, given the vagaries of the archaeological record. There is, however, one aspect of demography we can estimate using archaeological data—the number of individuals composing each household.

Recently, southeastern archaeologists have used a variety of methods for estimating household size based on the floor area of domestic structures (e.g., Scarry 1995; Smith 1995; Sullivan 1989, 1995). These methods are similar to each other and are based on the simple correlation of house size and the size of coresidential domestic groups identified by modern ethnographic studies (e.g., Casselberry 1974; Cook 1972; Hassan 1981). I calculate the household size for the Townsend structures using Casselberry's (1974) formula (household size [in persons] = $\frac{1}{6}$ floor area [in m^2]) in order to provide results that are comparable to the calculations provided by Sullivan (1989, 1995) for Cherokee and Mississippian households in eastern Tennessee. Also following Sullivan, I only include winter houses in the calculation of household size. Summer houses are not included in the calculations because they were ancillary domestic structures.

Given the distribution of structures across the project area, it can be safely assumed that there were six discrete households—three of these households consisted of paired winter and summer dwellings; one household consisted of a winter dwelling, a summer dwelling, and a ramada; and two households consisted of single winter houses. Unfortunately, the lack of definition of Household 5 (the household containing Structure 27) precludes calculating the size of this household. The household size estimates calculated using the Townsend architectural data are similar across the five households, ranging from six to eight people per household (Table 5.1). These figures are consistent with Sullivan's (1995:Table 5-1) estimates of household size at Chota-Tanasee and with the argument that the Cherokee households at Townsend likely comprised nuclear families.

Assessing the Occupation Duration of Houses at Townsend

Many of the current models used to estimate the occupation duration of houses are founded on structure longevity and the processes of architectural deterioration associated with the environment and insect infestation (e.g., McIntosh 1974; Moore and Gasco 1990; Warrick 1988). These models offer baseline estimates for structure longevity based on the use lives of particular architectural materials in certain environments. Typically, the occupation duration of a structure is estimated by combining these estimates with archaeological evidence of remodeling and/or rebuilding. For example, using architectural data from a continuously occupied residential zone in the American Bottom region, Pauketat (2003) derived estimates for the occupation duration of Mississippian period houses by determining the maximum number of rebuilding episodes that were present during each of the site's 50- to 75-year-long occupational phases. By dividing the occupational phase length by the maximum number of rebuilding episodes, Pauketat (2003:46) estimated that Mississippian structures in this region would have needed major repair or replacement after approximately 12 years. For this style of Mississippian period house, counting rebuilding episodes is relatively easy, as rebuilding most often involved the in situ replacement of entire walls. Cherokee architecture, however, was based on a different architectural vernacular in which repair involved individual post replacement rather than the replacement of entire wall sections (Wilson 2008:80). Thus, an entirely different method for estimating structure longevity and occupation duration is called for.

A promising method for estimating the occupation duration of Cherokee structures is the wall post replacement estimation method developed by

Gary Warrick (1988) for Iroquois longhouse structures. Warrick's (1988:34) method presents a very straightforward way to quantify the relationship between wall post density and occupation duration in structures in which repair proceeded through individual post replacement. Essentially, the model assumes that the total number of postholes encountered in the archaeological record equals the sum of the original number of wall posts comprising a structure and the number of posts used to replace rotten or deteriorated posts during the occupation of the structure. In order to calculate the occupation duration of a structure using Warrick's method, the analyst needs to know three pieces of information: (1) the type of wood the wall posts are made of, (2) the deterioration rate of that type of wood, and (3) the number of original wall posts comprising the structure (Warrick 1988:35–37). Except in rare cases where the charred remains of wall posts are found, archaeologists must calculate estimates using a number of different types of wood. Baseline data for determining the deterioration rates of wall posts can be found in a number of related studies concerning the use life of untreated fence posts (e.g., Blew and Kulp 1964; Krzyzewski et al. 1980; Purslow 1976). When analyzing the posthole patterns of Cherokee structures, it is impossible to know for certain which postholes represent original wall posts and which represent repair or replacement posts. As a way to circumvent this problem, Warrick (1988:40) recommends using the structure with the lowest wall post density in the sample as a proxy for the original number of wall posts in a structure.

Estimating the occupation duration of a particular structure proceeds in three steps. First, determine the wall post density of the structure in terms of wall posts per linear meter. This is done by dividing the total number of exterior wall posts by the circumference of the structure. Second, divide this value by the wall post density value representing the original number of posts (i.e., that from the structure with the lowest wall post density in the sample). The resulting ratio measures the proportion of wall posts that have been added to the structure (e.g., a value of 1.5 indicates that 50 percent of the wall posts have been replaced). Third, apply this ratio value to use-life curves calculated for different types of wood in order to attain an estimate of elapsed time (Warrick 1988:Figure 3).

A few changes are necessary in order to make this method more applicable to Cherokee structure data. First, estimates of occupation duration are limited to winter houses because wall post density values for summer houses evince a great deal of stochastic variation. Second, in the attempt to make the occupation duration estimates as robust as possible, the sample used in this study includes data from four of the Townsend structures as well as 18 clearly defined Cherokee winter houses uncovered at a number of other late seventeenth- and eighteenth-century Cherokee sites (Table 5.2). Lastly, new average use-life estimates and use-life curves have been calculated. Warrick's (1988:Table 5, Figure 3) use-life estimates are based on tree species commonly used in the Northeast, not the Southeast; furthermore, the use-life estimates he employs are based on fence post tests conducted primarily in the Midwest and Northeast. In order to provide more accurate estimates in this study, the wood types are limited to species commonly used in prehistoric southeastern architecture, namely ash, white oak, hickory, and southern yellow pine, and the average use-life estimates are calculated solely from fence post studies conducted in southeastern environmental settings (Blew and Kulp 1964; Marcoux 2008:Table 7.4). Use-life curves for southeastern wood types are created using a formula derived from a use-life study of over 50,000 railroad ties (MacLean 1926) (Figure 5.4).

Occupation duration estimates for the 22 Cherokee winter houses in the sample were calculated following the procedure outlined above and are given in Table 5.2. Wall post density values for each structure are based on published data and/or are calculated from published scale drawings (Howard 1997; Keel 1976; Polhemus 1987; Russ and Chapman 1983; Schroedl 1994; Schroedl, ed. 1986). For each structure, occupation duration estimates are obtained by applying the ratio of observed wall post density to original wall post density to the use-life curves of the wood types in Figure 5.4. Taking the wall post density ratio of Townsend Structure 22 as an example, the occupation duration estimates are found on the y-axis where the ratio value (1.52 on the x-axis) intercepts the use-life curves of the different wood types. In this example, the occupation duration estimate is 8 to 10 years if the structure was made of ash or white oak and 2 to 4 years for hickory or pine. The Townsend houses all have similar duration estimates spanning 2 to 12 years, depending on the building material. Indeed, with the exception of three houses, the results of this analysis strongly suggest that most Cherokee winter houses were occupied for less than a decade. While some degree of repair was evident in most structures, these results indicate that structures were rarely occupied for long enough to replace all of the wall posts. It is interesting that this pattern of short-term occupation applies broadly across different types of communities—from isolated farmsteads like the household at the Alarka site, to the small hamlet-sized community represented by the Townsend site, to households at large towns like Chota-Tanasee. As will be discussed below, this occupational pattern stands in sharp contrast to that of households from the preceding Mississippian period.

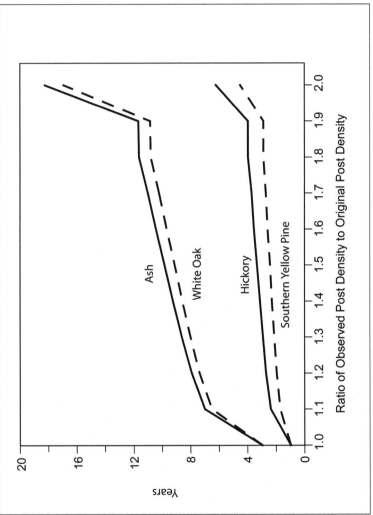

Figure 5.4. Use-life curves for untreated fence posts made from common southeastern trees (see also Warrick 1988 for use-life curves for fence posts made from northeastern trees). The x-axis measures the proportion of wall posts that have been replaced in any given house. A value of 1 represents a house with no replaced wall posts, while a value of 2 represents a house with all of its wall posts replaced (calculated using use-life curve in MacLean 1926).

Table 5.2. Estimated occupation duration for Cherokee winter houses

Site	Structure	Circumference (m)	Linear Wall Post Density (posts/m)	Observed Wall Post Density/ Original Wall Post Density	Estimated Occupation Duration (yrs)			
					Ash	White Oak	Hickory	Yellow Pine
Townsend[a]	8	23.20	1.03	1.34	8–10	6–8	2–4	2–4
	12	25.29	1.46	1.90	10–12	10–12	4–6	2–4
	22	24.65	1.18	1.52	8–10	8–10	2–4	2–4
	47	22.54	1.29	1.67	10–12	8–10	2–4	2–4
Chattooga	1	23.56	1.06	1.37	8–10	8–10	2–4	2–4
	2	21.99	1.09	1.41	8–10	8–10	2–4	2–4
Alarka	1	23.20	1.25	1.62	10–12	8–10	2–4	2–4
Tuckaseegee	1	22.02	.77[b]	1.00	2–4	2–4	0–2	0–2
Chota	6	20.10	1.94	2.51	>20	18–20	8–10	6–8
	10	22.98	.87	1.13	6–8	6–8	2–4	0–2
	12	22.02	.95	1.24	8–10	6–8	2–4	2–4
	14	18.19	.88	1.14	6–8	6–8	2–4	0–2
	15	21.06	.81	1.05	4–6	4–6	0–2	0–2

16	21.06	1.14	1.48	8-10	8-10	2-4	2-4
18	22.59	1.06	1.38	8-10	8-10	2-4	2-4
25	22.02	.95	1.24	8-10	6-8	2-4	2-4
27	21.06	1.04	1.35	8-10	8-10	2-4	2-4
Tanasee 3	21.06	1.28	1.66	10-12	8-10	2-4	2-4
5	21.06	1.14	1.48	8-10	8-10	2-4	2-4
Mialoquo 1	22.50	1.29	1.67	10-12	8-10	2-4	2-4
Toqua 59	19.62	1.88	2.44	>20	18-20	8-10	6-8
104	19.15	2.19	2.64	>20	18-20	8-10	6-8

[a]Structure 1 was not included in the sample because the northeastern portion of its posthole pattern was heavily disturbed.
[b]This wall post density value was used as a proxy for the original wall post density of Cherokee winter houses in the calculations of occupation duration.

Assessing the Occupation Duration from Pit Features

Occupation duration can also be assessed by examining the use life and abandonment of pit features (e.g., DeBoer 1988; Dickens 1985; Koldehoff and Galloy 2006; Ward 1985; Wesson 1999). Excavations at the Townsend site identified 31 refuse-filled basin and pit features associated with the late seventeenth- and early eighteenth-century Cherokee occupation (Figure 5.5). Examining the morphological and pottery refuse data from all Cherokee basin and pit features at Townsend, I find that the Townsend households did not rely heavily on subterranean pits to store their foodstuffs and that the pits had relatively short use lives.

The distribution of pit feature volumes at Townsend reveals the existence of three well-defined size classes. Figure 5.6 is a histogram depicting the volume estimates for all of the basins and pits associated with the Cherokee occupation at Townsend. The distribution of these measures is clearly trimodal, with classes composed of basins and pits with volumes of less than 150 L, basins and pits with volumes between 175 and 325 L, and pits with volumes between 400 and 500 L. A more detailed picture emerges when feature morphology is considered along with volume. A scatter plot diagram depicting maximum diameter and volume shows four clusters of values (Figure 5.7). The cluster containing features with the smallest diameter and volume values (i.e., those closest to the scatter plot origin) is overwhelmingly composed of pits located inside of Cherokee structures. Moving to the right, one encounters a group of small basins and pits that are similar in volume but different in terms of shape. The five features forming the upper branch of the group are narrower and deeper than those in the lower branch, which are broad and shallow. The lower branch may be the remnants of larger features that were truncated by historic plowing. Medium basins and pits form a relatively coherent cluster, and the location of large pits in the scatter plot clearly identifies them as a separate size class.

A comparison of basins and pits among the six Townsend households is presented in Table 5.3. The distribution of feature size classes among the households varies greatly. Medium and small features were common in all households, and three of the six households had large pits. Only two households had interior pits—all but one of these were associated with Household 4. Also, a great deal of variability is present in the number of features associated with each household and their combined volume. The most likely reasons for such variability include differences in household occupation duration and/or sample size differences due to historic disturbances and boundary issues associated with the limits of excavation. Interestingly, the median and mean measures for feature volume evince much

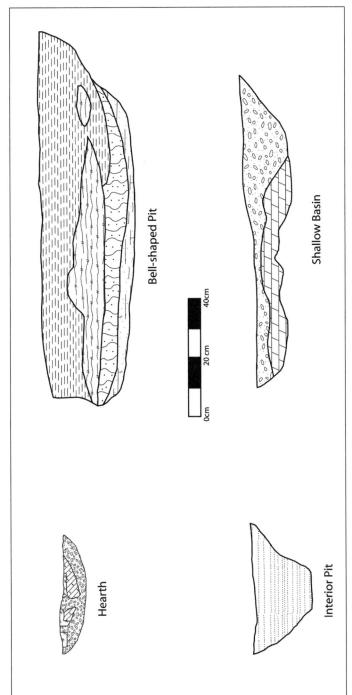

Figure 5.5. Examples of four feature types found in household contexts at Townsend.

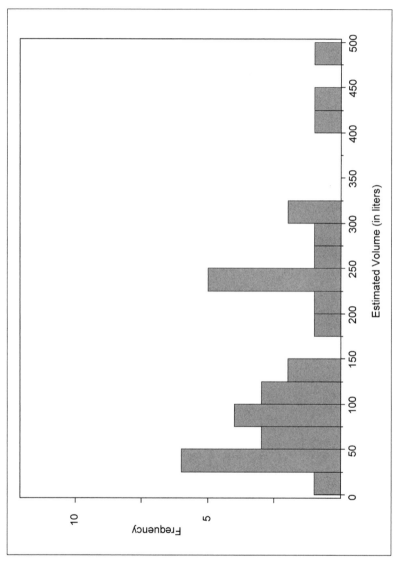

Figure 5.6. Histogram depicting the distribution of volume among basin and pit features associated with Townsend households.

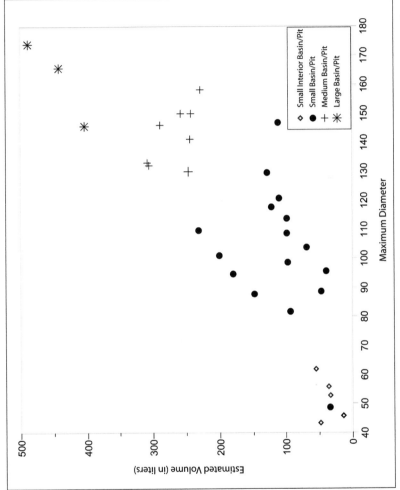

Figure 5.7. Scatter plot depicting the relationship between maximum feature diameter and estimated volume.

Table 5.3. Comparison of feature size classes and feature volume among Townsend households

Household	Large Basins/Pits	Medium Basins/Pits	Small Basins/Pits	Small Interior Basins/Pits	Combined Volume (L)	Median Volume (L)	Mean Volume (L)
1	1	4	5	0	2,017	187.81	201.75
2	0	2	1	1	692	184.30	173.00
3	1	1	2	0	882	200.15	220.39
4	1	1	2	4	1,176	52.20	138.04
5	0	0	2	0	438	219.11	219.11
6	0	0	3	0	213	97.22	71.05

less variability across households. This suggests that while the composition of household storage facilities varied greatly in terms of size and number of individual basins and pits, the underlying storage capacity of each household was similar—and it was not particularly large, especially when compared with the storage capacity of later eighteenth-century Cherokee households. These later households featured new forms of subterranean storage and increases in feature volume on the order of two to three times (Marcoux 2008:346, Table 7.9). This difference is telling of a significant transformation that occurred in Cherokee storage practices following the English Contact period, perhaps associated with a growing reliance on root crops like sweet potatoes (Riggs, personal communication 2007).

A very rough relative estimate for the use life of Cherokee basins and pits at Townsend can be arrived at using qualitative data. Researchers documenting the importance of subterranean storage to prehistoric and historic southeastern Indian communities have identified markers that can be used to assess the relative use life of features based on their stratigraphy (DeBoer 1988:4; Koldehoff and Galloy 2006:285–286; Wesson 1999:151). Specifically, these researchers equate a long use life with a feature's being open (i.e., unfilled) for a relatively long period of time or a feature's evincing multiple uses over a long period of time. The correlate of the first part of the definition is seen archaeologically in a very distinct type of stratigraphy known as slumping. This is caused by the erosion of the basin or pit wall resulting from sediments being carried into an open feature by wind, water, or human activity. The second indication is the presence of multiple stratigraphic zones, indicating several filling episodes (artifact-bearing soils) separated by periods of abandonment and inactivity (culturally sterile soils).

Neither of these indicators of long use life is common at Townsend. Of the 31 pit features in the Townsend sample, five show evidence of slumping or slope wash. These include one small interior pit and four medium-sized features. Moreover, 28 of the 31 features contain only one or two stratigraphic zones, and no feature profile evinces the distinctive alternating pattern of filling and inactivity that is associated with a long use life. Taken together, these patterns point to relatively short use lives for most Cherokee basins and pits and support the interpretation that basins and pits were probably not used for any sort of long-term storage of food or other material. Indeed, only two bell-shaped pits, a morphological form closely associated with food storage in ethnohistoric accounts and archaeological contexts (DeBoer 1988), are associated with the Cherokee occupation at Townsend. Both of these pits are smaller (i.e., <250 L) than the average Woodland period bell-shaped pits cited by DeBoer (1988) (300–500 L).

Furthermore, potsherd density in these pits is quite low across all basins and pits. The majority of the features contain fewer than .5 sherds per liter of fill and the highest recorded value is only 1.5 sherds per liter. This suggests that Townsend house sites were not occupied for sufficient time for surface middens to accumulate (see Shumate et al. 2005 for a similar situation).

CHANGES IN DOMESTIC SPACE AND TIME IN THE DAILY LIVES OF ENGLISH CONTACT PERIOD CHEROKEE HOUSEHOLDS

Recent studies of southeastern Mississippian sites such as Moundville, Coweeta Creek, and Town Creek have demonstrated that these communities featured highly structured and long-lived residential areas created by the building, repairing, and/or rebuilding of houses within the same spatial footprint (e.g., Boudreaux 2007; Rodning 2002, 2004, 2007; Wilson 2005, 2008). To the authors of these studies, the repeated use of domestic space over the course of decades reflects the recursive formation of household identities through the creation of long-term spatial "histories." In contrast, the rapidly changing conditions of the late seventeenth and early eighteenth centuries outlined in Chapter 2 simply did not allow for the creation of strong sedimented community and household identities rooted in the *longue durée* of daily repetition, history, and memory. Quite the opposite, this environment required strategies that were the very antitheses of those that constituted Mississippian identity—short-term strategies that emphasized flexibility and improvisation. This shift in the strategies of Cherokee households can be identified in the archaeological record as dramatic changes in community organization and architectural vernacular.

The notion that southeastern Indian groups altered the spatial organization of their communities in the wake of European contact is not new. Indeed, numerous studies of historic Creek and Cherokee community organization have noted a shift from highly structured, densely settled fortified villages during the sixteenth and early seventeenth centuries to sprawling and sparsely settled unfortified villages and scattered "plantations" during the late seventeenth and eighteenth centuries (Ashley 1988; Rodning 2004; Schroedl 2000; Schroedl, ed. 1986; Waselkov 1990; Wesson 1999, 2008; see Chicken 1916 [1725]:101; Long 1969 [1725]:34–36 for period accounts of Cherokee community organization). While houses in South Appalachian Mississippian and Protohistoric period villages, such as the Rymer site in eastern Tennessee, the King site in northeast Georgia, and the Coweeta Creek site in western North Carolina, were often spaced less than 15 m apart, houses in later Cherokee communities, such as the Townsend site and the Chota-Tanasee site, were spaced from 25 to 50 m apart.

Researchers have also recognized that domestic structures in the southern Appalachian region underwent a significant transformation during the seventeenth century (Hally 2002; Waselkov 1990). For this study, I synthesize published data associated with two architectural variables, method of manufacture and repair and structural robusticity. I use these data to compare a sample of 26 late seventeenth- and eighteenth-century Cherokee winter houses with a sample of 23 late sixteenth- and early seventeenth-century South Appalachian Mississippian structures (Appendix B) (Hally 1988; Howard 1997; Keel 1976; Polhemus 1987; Rodning 2004; Russ and Chapman 1983; Schroedl 1994; Schroedl, ed. 1986).

I assess the methods used to manufacture the domestic structures in the sample through the consideration of structure shape, the configuration of the structural posts, and the number of structural posts. The most obvious difference between Mississippian structures and Cherokee structures is shape (Figure 5.8). While all but one of the Mississippian structures in the sample are square with rounded corners, all of the Cherokee winter houses are circular or octagonal. Mississippian houses and Cherokee houses also differ in the style of their entryways. Mississippian houses typically feature wall-trench entryways, while historic Cherokee winter houses employ a simple opening and wind baffle. The basic arrangement of posts in both Mississippian and Cherokee structures includes large-diameter, deeply set central roof support posts, exterior wall posts, and interior posts that presumably supported benches or formed interior partitions. The similar arrangement of posts suggests that both types of structures are based on the same rigid-post architectural vernacular (Hally 2002).

Another dimension of variability in construction methods is structural robusticity, which can be measured as a post density ratio of the total number of posts composing a structure to that structure's floor area. At first glance, there are vast differences between Mississippian and Cherokee houses in terms of this value; however, much of this difference is due to the fact that Mississippian houses were much more frequently rebuilt in the same location (see below). In order to control for the difference in in situ rebuilding, the comparison of post density ratios is limited to structures with a single hearth. For Mississippian structures in North Carolina and Alabama, Rodning (2004) and Wilson (2005, 2008) have recognized a correspondence between the number of times a hearth was remodeled and the number of times a structure was rebuilt. Consequently, structures with one hearth should represent houses with relatively short occupation

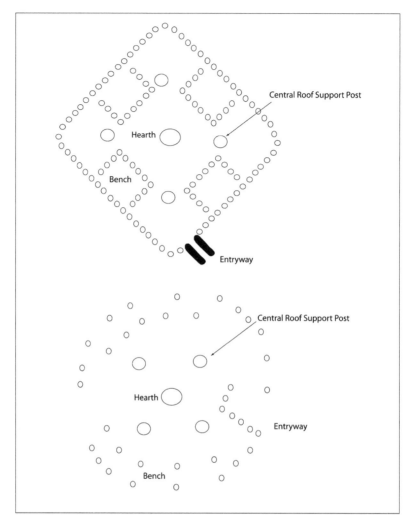

Figure 5.8. Schematic comparison of Mississippian house (top) and Cherokee winter house (bottom). (Drawing of Mississippian house adapted from
Rodning 2004:Figure 5.2.)

spans. While the reduced sample is somewhat smaller than is desired (n =
24), a comparison reveals that non-rebuilt Mississippian houses contain
a significantly greater number of posts per square meter than non-rebuilt
Cherokee winter houses (Figure 5.9). Indeed, the median post density ratio for Mississippian houses (median = 4.31 posts/m^2) is over two and a half
times greater than that of Cherokee winter houses (median = 1.53 posts/m^2).
Given that the structures from the two periods were built using the same

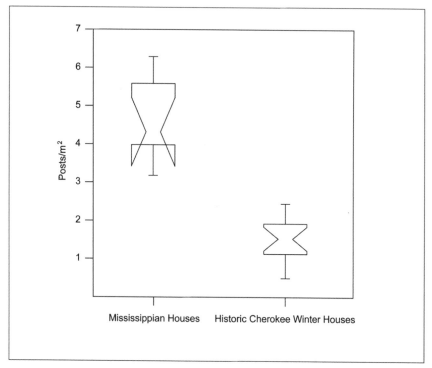

Figure 5.9. Boxplots comparing post densities between non-rebuilt Mississippian houses and non-rebuilt historic Cherokee winter houses. Note: the "folded" appearance of the boxplot is due to small sample size and indicates that the 95-percent confidence interval of the median is greater than the H-spread.

rigid-post architectural principles, this difference suggests a significant change in methods of manufacture—a good deal more material and energy were involved in constructing the Mississippian house form than the later Cherokee house form.

Although the methods of manufacture of domestic structures changed from the late sixteenth to the late seventeenth century, structure size (and consequently household size) appears to have remained stable. The mean floor area of Mississippian houses in the study sample is 41.03 m², while that of Cherokee winter houses is 38.12 m². Similar floor area estimates for historic and prehistoric domestic structures have been reported by Sullivan (1995:115) and Hally (2002:107). These figures suggest an average household size of seven individuals for the Mississippian period and six individuals for the historic period. Such a small difference in floor area is more likely related to the architectural differences between Mississippian and Cherokee houses rather than to actual differences in household size.

Differences in post density also suggest that Cherokee households enacted significant changes in the methods they used to repair domestic structures. Even a cursory glance at the plan view drawings of houses at Mississippian towns like Coweeta Creek and Cherokee towns like Chota reveals major differences in the density of posthole patterns (e.g., Rodning 2002: Figure 2; Schroedl, ed. 1986:Figure 1.31). As I will discuss shortly, the differences doubtless result from differences in occupation duration, but they are also due in part to the use of two different repair techniques. These techniques have been identified by Wilson (2008:80) in his study of Mississippian architecture at the Moundville site in Alabama. The first technique involves the complete rebuilding of the entire structure in situ, while the second technique involves the repair of particular architectural elements. The palimpsests of postholes at Mississippian sites across the southern Appalachian region suggest that most of these houses were entirely rebuilt in situ (Hally 1988, 2002; Polhemus 1987; Rodning 2004:152; Sullivan 1989, 1995). By contrast, the posthole patterns of Cherokee houses suggest that rebuilding occurred gradually through the repair of individual posts rather than periodic complete rebuilding. When considered together with the difference in structure robusticity, this pattern indicates that late seventeenth- and eighteenth-century Cherokee households were making the strategic choice not to invest time and energy in a long-term occupation. A comparison of occupation duration estimates for Mississippian and Cherokee houses supports this argument.

The occupation duration of houses is a very important yet seldom-considered variable in southeastern archaeology (notable exceptions include Cook 2007 and Pauketat 1989, 2003:40). Indeed, this dimension represents the most significant source of difference between Mississippian and Cherokee houses. Given the differences in repair technique between Mississippian and Cherokee houses, a different method must be used to compare occupation duration. One solution is to use a more general measure of post density as an alternative proxy for repair and rebuilding (see also Cook 2007). This proxy, which is a simple ratio of total posts to the floor area of each structure (posts/square meter), has a strong positive correlation with the linear wall post density measure used above to estimate Cherokee house occupation duration ($r = .67$). The correlation suggests that the posts/square meter post density variable can also be used to measure occupation duration, at least relatively. In addition to using a different post density proxy, comparisons of occupation duration between Mississippian and Cherokee houses must also take into account large differences in the initial number of posts used to construct each type of house. This is ac-

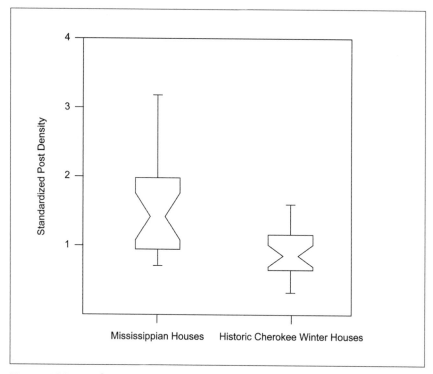

Figure 5.10. Boxplots comparing standardized post density measures between Mississippian houses and historic Cherokee winter houses. Standardization involved dividing the post density values of each Mississippian and Cherokee house by the median post density measures of non-rebuilt houses for each group.

complished through standardization by dividing the post density value of each house by the appropriate median post density value calculated for single building episodes of Mississippian (4.31 posts/m^2) and Cherokee (1.53 posts/m^2) houses.

The comparison of the standardized post density values indicates that the occupation duration of Mississippian houses is significantly greater than that of Cherokee winter houses (Figure 5.10). Unfortunately, unlike Warrick's (1988) method this method does not result in occupation duration estimates expressed in actual years; however, the results still speak to large relative differences in occupation spans, with the median values hinting that the occupation duration of Mississippian houses was twice that of Cherokee houses. Much longer occupation durations for Mississippian houses are further supported by evidence for multiple remodeling episodes of central hearths and entryways in Mississippian houses (Rodning 2007) and the absence of this type of repair in the Cherokee houses included in this sample.

DISCUSSION

What forces could be behind such a radical shift in settlement strategies? Rodning (2004:418–419) suggests that resource depletion might have caused the eventual shift in settlement patterns among the Cherokee. Recent geographic information system (GIS) modeling of resources and Cherokee town location, however, has found that the Cherokee population would never have risen to levels that would have endangered natural resources (Bolstad and Gragson 2008). Ashley (1988), Waselkov (1990), and Wesson (2008) propose that Creek communities shifted to a dispersed settlement pattern as a response to the burgeoning trade in deerskins. These researchers argue that as Creek households became increasingly engaged in the trade, they moved to areas that were better positioned to exploit trading opportunities, as well as to escape the building hegemony of elites within villages.

Given the violent historical context of the English Contact period, it is interesting that the raids associated with the Indian slave trade are rarely discussed as an influencing factor for this shift in community organization. In the Northeast, the shift to a dispersed community pattern has been argued to be a counter to this type of "skulking" warfare (Ferguson and Whitehead 1992; Lee 2004; Malone 1991). Indeed, the journal of George Chicken records a Cherokee headman stating that their strategy to deal with Creek raids would be "to lett them come to their Towns, but not undiscovered, for they design to give them a Smash in their Towns First and then to gather all their Strength and follow them when they are upon retreat with their Wounded men" (Chicken 1916 [1725]:156). We get another description of this type of attack/counterattack skirmishing from Major John Norton's journal:

> From this period [ca. 1710] we seldom hear of the Five Nations being engaged with the French or Northern Tribes . . . The Warriors sought fame to the South of the Ohio, in desultory excursions against the Cherokee and Catawbas . . . The Nottowegui Warriors left home in parties from two hundred to ten . . . [they traveled until they] came upon the Head Waters of Holston, along the Banks of which the Cherokee Hunters were frequently scattered;—these they often surprised, killing and taking them prisoners. At other times, they proceeded to the Villages, but only in small parties to prevent discovery,—the Main Body gener-

ally remaining on the Big Sandy, Holston or in some other part of the country which they then called the Middle Grounds,—and which is now fallen in the State of Kentucky . . . When the party detached, had gained Scalps or Prisoners, they fled to where their comrades awaited for their return, to support them in case they might be surprised by superior force [Norton 1970 (1816):262].

From these accounts, it is clear the Cherokee strategy to combat enemy raids was to trap their enemy within their town and then counterattack. A dispersed community organization would allow for setting this trap while at the same time not exposing as many people to the raid as would a densely settled town.

Space and time are the two most fundamental dimensions explored by archaeologists. Rather than use these dimensions as etic constructs to explore life in the past, we can achieve a much richer understanding by showing how the dimensions themselves were strategically manipulated by households. Scholars have done so with domestic spaces within Mississippian period communities, demonstrating that they were highly structured *and* multigenerational (Hally and Kelly 1998; Rodning 2002, 2004, 2007; Wilson 2005, 2008). Rodning (2007:477), for example, argues that the redundancy of in situ household rebuilding and continuity in the town plan of the Coweeta Creek site bespeak the importance each house held as an anchor for household and community identity. In stark contrast to these patterns, my analyses show that Cherokee community organization was much less structured. Furthermore, I find that members of Cherokee communities were not investing as much time or energy in the initial construction or repair of their houses and that the domestic footprint of houses in Cherokee communities was rarely occupied for more than a decade. I believe these patterns suggest that the seventeenth century heralded the disintegration of the physical house as a material "anchor" for the social group. Interestingly, Rodning's (2004, 2007, 2009) study of the Coweeta Creek site suggests that during this period public buildings (i.e., townhouses) may have begun to fill this role.

We must not underestimate the importance of time (and timing) in historical process. Here, I am thinking about time as the tempo and rhythm of daily life that gives direction and structure to daily practices and, as such, constitutes their meaning (Bourdieu 1977:8–9). The results of my study suggest that time can have a particular direction and scale. For Mississippian households engaged in the creation of deeply rooted historical identities through the building and rebuilding of houses, daily life appears to have emphasized references to the past, and time appears to have been reckoned on the order of decades or even centuries (Rodning 2007; Wilson 2008; see also papers in Beck 2007). In sharp contrast, the chaotic social, political, and economic landscape of the late seventeenth and early eighteenth centuries necessitated a radical yet strategic shift away from household practices emphasizing continuity with the past and toward those aimed at negotiating an uncertain future.

6

Conclusions

At its core, this study has been about the impact of culture contact on southeastern Indian communities during the late seventeenth and early eighteenth centuries. It is part of a long tradition of research in both history and archaeology that extends back well over a century (e.g., Crane 2004; Ethridge 2006; Mooney 1900; Schroedl 2000; Schroedl, ed. 1986; Smith 1987; Swanton 1998; Ward and Davis 2001; Worth 2006). This tradition focuses on culture change within Indian communities, the impetus of which is attributed (to a greater or lesser extent) to the effects of disease, warfare, and interaction with European traders. My study is no different in this sense. Certainly, these historical forces were paramount in shaping the histories of all Indian communities in the Southeast during the English Contact period, and to deny their pervasiveness would be folly. There is an equal danger, however, in relying too heavily upon such generalized historical forces, for they gloss over important details that are crucial to achieving a nuanced understanding of the period on a local level. From the outset, I have attempted to avoid these interpretive pitfalls by approaching the topics of culture contact and culture change in southeastern Indian communities from a novel perspective.

Following the most recent historical scholarship addressing the English Contact period in the Southeast, I have stressed the importance of local interactions, contingencies, and the active role of Indian groups in forging their histories. I also departed from past archaeological studies of Cherokee communities by eschewing the topics of "O"rigins and "A"cculturation, choosing rather to frame my research with theories that stress the agency of small groups, specifically Cherokee households and their ability to adapt to the social, political, and economic disruptions of the period through the actions of daily life. I chose as a case study a community that was all but unknown to Europeans. Nevertheless, I was able to demonstrate that significant and strategic changes could be identified in the daily lives of households—*sui generis* changes that had little or no direct link to European contact.

Constructing a Historical Narrative
for the Tuckaleechee Towns

Now, to return to the question posed at the beginning of this book, how would a narrative of daily life during the English Contact period read for the everyday folk living in the households of the Tuckaleechee Towns? This study offers a number of new insights that can aid us in constructing such a narrative. The backdrop for this narrative is the chaotic landscape of the southeastern shatter zone (Chapter 2). History tells us (or rather suggests by omission) that initially most Cherokee communities intentionally avoided direct contact with Europeans. There are hints in historical documents, however, indicating that in spite of this strategy the shock waves of violence and disease nevertheless penetrated into Cherokee communities in the form of slave raids and epidemics. As in numerous examples across the region, the households of the Tuckaleechee Towns were simply trying to adapt to this new and uncertain reality while fulfilling the necessities of daily life.

While additional archaeological research is needed to better characterize late prehistoric and Contact period occupations in the Little River valley, at this point it appears that the individuals who lived at Townsend were relatively recent immigrants to Tuckaleechee Cove. There are Mississippian period occupations in the valley at the Townsend site and downstream at another site (40Bt47), but these are much earlier settlements dating to the twelfth century (Bentz and Greene 1991). Currently, no late prehistoric or protohistoric occupations are known (Cornett, personal communication 2007). Hence, while admittedly tenuous, the current evidence suggests that the late seventeenth- and/or early eighteenth-century occupation at Townsend had no immediate predecessor.

Aside from the obviously picturesque setting admired by Timberlake (2001 [1762]:118–119), Tuckaleechee Cove offered prospective Cherokee settlers a strategic spot for establishing a community. The cove features a broad alluvial valley suitable for extensive agriculture and could easily have supported a town-sized population. Furthermore, this fertile floodplain is surrounded by a continuous wall of mountains, making entrance to the cove very difficult except through the narrow passes where the Little River and its tributaries flow. While well protected, the cove was definitely not isolated; rather, it was connected to Indian towns to the north and Cherokee settlements to the south by two major trading paths (Figure 3.2). For a group of emigrant (most likely displaced) Cherokee families seeking a protected location in which to establish a community, the decision to settle in Tuckaleechee Cove would have been elementary.

The collection of families that established households at the Townsend site in Tuckaleechee Cove formed an "improvised community." On a literal level, the Townsend householders were part of an improvised community in the sense that this new settlement was a coalescent society comprised of emigrants from different parts of Cherokee territory (Hudson 2002; Kowalewski 2006). That the clutch of households excavated at the Townsend site were of disparate geographic origins is clear in the fact that they practiced quite distinct regional potting traditions (Chapter 4). Two of the households practiced a tradition with ties to the Overhill Towns in the lower Tennessee River valley, and one household's tradition is clearly identified with the Middle, Out, and Lower towns. It is plausible that the members of these households, or at least the potters of the households, immigrated to Tuckaleechee Cove from these two regions. The remaining three households practiced a tradition that has not previously been recognized archaeologically. Given the absence of this tradition at sites located within the Cherokee territory of the eighteenth century, one is tempted to look to oral history and place its origins in the Nolichucky River valley (Hicks 1826; Smith 1987). Until we conduct further research into the ceramic chronology of this region, however, such an attribution would be pure speculation. Another explanation, which is equally speculative at this point, is that the tradition associated with Tuckaleechee series pottery was a local development. If this were the case, then such a tradition would represent the materialization of a newly forming identity—one that expressed the solidarity of the householders living in Tuckaleechee Cove.

On a more theoretical level, the community was improvised in the same way that all communities are continually constituted through daily practice (Anderson 1991; Joyce and Hendon 2000; Norval 1996; Watanabe 1992; Yaeger and Canuto 2000). As a newly formed community, one can imagine that much was "on the table" and open to negotiation with regard to social and political structure, as well as the basic issues that affected the households collectively. Cooperation in planting, harvesting, foraging, and hunting; mutual protection; courtship, marriage, and child care; dispute resolution; and a host of other matters had to be dealt with. Consequently, improvisation would doubtless have been necessary on a daily basis as these newly acquainted folk worked out their social, political, and economic relationships. Recently, Rodning (2004, 2009) has characterized the integrative role played by townhouses in Cherokee communities as focal points of collective ritual and public discourse. Presently, no townhouses have been identified archaeologically in Tuckaleechee Cove; however, given the importance of these structures in most Cherokee towns, it is likely that one or more did exist.

Life in Tuckaleechee Cove involved the same domestic tasks that had marked the quotidian existence of households for centuries. Farming, pottery and tool manufacturing, hunting, cooking, child care, building and repairing houses—these tasks still filled the day; however, because of the unique historical context of the shatter zone, some fundamental aspects of daily life between 1650 and 1715 were very different. Architectural data indicate that the Cherokee householders in Tuckaleechee Cove dramatically altered the spacing and tempo of daily life, shifting to an extensive, widely spaced community layout and shortening household tenure within a given space (Chapter 5). While not framed in the same manner as I have done in this study, this reshaping of the basic structuring forces of daily life is a pattern that one sees repeated in English Contact period Indian communities across the Southeast (e.g., Ashley 1988; Rodning 2004; Schroedl 1986, 2000; Waselkov 1990; Wesson 1999, 2008). Given the pervasiveness of these changes, I believe that this period marks a major *strategic* departure from the life of Mississippian households a century earlier. While the dense and orderly South Appalachian Mississippian towns with their durable public and domestic spaces evoke the notion of permanence (Rodning 2007), one gets the opposite impression from the loosely ordered Cherokee towns with their lightly built and short-lived houses.

The apparent abandonment of this notion of permanence may reflect Cherokee householders' attempts to adapt to the frenetic historical forces of the English Contact period landscape. Certainly, a strategy stressing flexibility and improvisation would have provided a means to successfully negotiate the social, political, and economic uncertainty generated by the southeastern shatter zone. When viewed within this frame, the archaeological patterns I identified at Townsend make a good deal of sense. Flexibility and improvisation would definitely be required to make the decision to move away from one's town and into an unfamiliar region to live with a group of unrelated immigrant families. Furthermore, the changes in house construction and repair practices suggest that the relationships among Cherokee households, materialized in the tenure of their spatial associations, were more fleeting than those among Mississippian households. It could be that long-lasting household relationships were materialized in other ways during the English Contact period, such as in associations with a particular townhouse. Alternatively, we might speculate that the householders never intended that their relationships with other households would last generations. At the very least, we can say that identity in English Contact period Cherokee households was not incumbent upon the accumulation of a deep residential history (*sensu* Rodning 2007; Wilson 2005, 2008)—or that this type of identity construction simply was not possible for Cherokee households given the rapidly evolving landscape.

Just as the decision to settle in Tuckaleechee Cove was strategic, so too was the decision to abandon it. Currently, our understanding of this event is rather poor and will benefit from future archaeological surveys and excavations in the Little River valley and surrounding coves. Based on ceramic and glass trade bead data, the Townsend households all appear to be abandoned by ca. 1720 (Marcoux 2008). If we consult the Barnwell-Hammerton and Barnwell Manuscript maps, the latest date for abandonment can be pushed back to ca. 1715. Just prior to this date, there are accounts of heavy Iroquois raiding in Cherokee territory (Nairne 1988 [1708]:76; Norton 1970 [1816]:262). Given that the Tuckaleechee Towns were the northernmost Cherokee settlements and were located near the Great Indian Warpath, the inhabitants of these towns would have been among the first targets of Iroquois raiding parties. If this were the case, then the once advantageous location of Tuckaleechee Cove would have quickly become a deadly liability. Archaeological evidence of the Iroquois threat, however, is currently lacking. None of the households at Townsend appear to have been destroyed, and only two burials were identified in the excavations at the site. Of course, the Cherokee settlers could have abandoned Tuckaleechee Cove for a number of other reasons including disease, internal conflicts, or simple attrition. Consequently, while we are now definitely closer to solving Timberlake's mystery of why the Tuckaleechee Towns were abandoned, the definitive answer remains elusive.

ARCHAEOLOGY AND THE CHALLENGE OF THE HISTORICAL NARRATIVE

Rather than end this study with the call to use the findings as a general model to "explain" other archaeological examples, I will close by stressing the importance of historical contingency and the need to construct detailed historical narratives for each archaeological case. If the reader accepts my interpretation, the Townsend households were part of a short-lived coalescent community that was held together by flexibility, by improvisation, and most importantly by necessity. The Cherokee household occupations excavated at the Townsend site, however, only represent a snapshot of daily life for a small portion of one Tuckaleechee Town community. This narrative will likely change when more sites representing Tuckaleechee Town communities are identified and excavated.

As undocumented short-lived communities located outside of known Cherokee territory, the Tuckaleechee Towns represent at best faint "blips" existing at the fringes of our archaeological and historical knowledge. In fact, if it were not for federally mandated data recovery excavations at the Townsend site, these communities would still be outside of the focus of academic research. How many other Indian communities occupy a similar peripheral position in our developing understanding of the English Contact period? The number, I am sure, is larger than we think. This study demonstrates that we ignore these communities at our own peril, for they have the potential to provide powerful archaeological examples of historical processes that were definitional to the English Contact period (e.g., cultural adaptation and ethnogenesis). The historical narrative that I have presented for the Townsend site is one of hundreds that can and should be written for undocumented English Contact period Indian communities across the Southeast. I hope that this challenge will be taken up and that scholars will identify in the material residues of everyday life the myriad strategies of folk adapting to the trials and opportunities of the period. In doing so, they will contribute to and improve the grand historical narrative of the English Contact period started by Crane (2004) and Swanton (1998) over 75 years ago.

Appendix A
Statistical Methodology

DESCRIPTIVE STATISTICS

In this study, I utilize statistical measures and techniques associated with exploratory data analysis (EDA) rather than traditional significance testing statistical methods. I chose to use EDA methods and measures primarily because they are better suited to the constraints of archaeological data sets. EDA, as set forth by its founders John Tukey (1977) and Paul Velleman and David Hoaglin (1981), is an inductive approach that aims to identify structure in data sets through relatively simple techniques and with minimal prior assumptions. The techniques are particularly well suited to archaeological data sets because they are nonparametric (i.e., they do not require assumptions of normally distributed data), they are resistant to the effects of outlier values, and they emphasize pattern recognition through simple visual display.

One visual display technique appearing multiple times in this study is known as a notched boxplot (McGill et al. 1978; Velleman and Hoaglin 1981:65–81). Boxplots graphically represent the spread of particular values. Measures used in this study include temper particle size, sherd thickness, and structural post density. In notched boxplots, the median value is depicted as the center of the notch in each boxplot, and the length of the "box" represents the H-spread, or the range within which the central 50 percent of the values fall. The ends of this box are known as hinges, whose values are essentially equivalent to the first and third quartiles of the distribution. The vertical lines extending from the box, known as whiskers, mark values that fall within 1.5 H-spreads of the hinges. Outliers in the distributions are marked as asterisks and far-outliers as circles. The notches within the boxes represent the 95-percent confidence intervals for each median value. In using boxplots to compare the median values from different analytical groups, if the notched intervals around any medians do not overlap, one can be confident that those analytical groups are different at a .05 level of statistical significance.

Correspondence Analysis

I employ correspondence analysis (CA) in the ceramic analyses presented in Chapter 4. CA is a powerful multivariate statistical technique that has been used widely for seriating artifact assemblages in European archaeology (e.g., Bech 1988; Madsen 1988). One rarely sees CA, however, in the archaeological literature of North America (see Duff 1996 for a notable exception). The relative obscurity of CA is curious given that the technique is based on straightforward and fundamental statistical logic—essentially the same logic that underlies the Chi-squared test. Unlike other multivariate techniques, it requires no assumptions of the data and works directly on untransformed artifact frequencies (counts); like the Chi-squared test, CA is resistant to differences in sample sizes.

One of the largest obstacles to investigating variability in the composition of pottery assemblages is finding a technique that can simultaneously account for variability along dozens of dimensions representing the different combinations of temper and exterior surface treatment—there are simply too many variables. Fortunately, CA excels at reducing the dimensionality of data matrices by measuring the associations among both cases (in Chapter 4, cases include household- and site-level pottery assemblages) and variables (in Chapter 4, variables include temper and exterior surface treatment combinations) simultaneously. CA solves the dilemma by providing the analyst with a way to visually explore and present multivariate data by reducing the dimensionality of a data matrix.

How CA reduces the dimensionality of a data matrix is a bit involved, but a brief discussion should suffice to make it clearer (see Baxter 1994 and Shennan 1997 for in-depth discussions of CA). CA can be viewed as a more complex Chi-squared test that compares all of the row and column profiles of a data matrix and computes the departure of each case and variable from an average profile. In this study, the average case profile would be a hypothetical pottery assemblage consisting of the average proportions of each pottery type, and the average column profile would simply be the average frequency of pottery types as calculated across all assemblages. In the biplot produced by CA, the average profiles are represented by the intersection of the x- and y-axes. Using simple Chi-squared calculations, CA measures both the degree and the direction of departure of each pottery assemblage and pottery type from the average profiles.

In this study, CA is carried out using the Correspondence Analysis module of the Bonn archaeological software package. This program takes input in the form of a frequency matrix and returns output in the form of distributional biplots and diagnostic statistics. One of the most useful results of this technique is a biplot that depicts the relative degree of association of household pottery assemblages, as well as of the different combinations of temper material and exterior surface treatments. In interpreting the biplots, one can infer (1) that the pottery types located near one another in the biplot typically occur together in the same contexts; (2) that contexts (e.g., Household 1, Household 2, etc.) located near one another have similar pottery assemblages (and vice versa); and (3) that the pottery types located near each household assemblage in the biplot represent the dominant types in each of those assemblages.

Appendix B
*Architectural Data for Cherokee
and Mississippian Structures*

Site	Structure	Period	Structure Shape	Number of Hearths[a]	Total Posts	Floor Area (m²)	Post Density (posts/m²)	Standardized Post Density[b]
Alarka	Sw273-1	Historic	Octagonal	1	98	40.00	2.45	1.60
Chattooga	Oc18-1	Historic	Circular	1	54[c]	40.00	1.35	.88
Chattooga	Oc18-2	Historic	Circular	1	80[c]	50.25	1.59	1.04
Chota	Mr2-1	Historic	Circular	1	40	36.88	1.08	.71
Chota	Mr2-5	Historic	Octagonal	1	33	38.55	.86	.56
Chota	Mr2-6	Historic	Octagonal	1	57	32.14	1.77	1.16
Chota	Mr2-10	Historic	Octagonal	0	57	41.99	1.36	.89
Chota	Mr2-12	Historic	Circular	0	48	38.55	1.24	.81
Chota	Mr2-14	Historic	Circular	0	26	33.54	.78	.51
Chota	Mr2-15	Historic	Octagonal	0	45	35.30	1.27	.83
Chota	Mr2-16	Historic	Circular	1	69	35.77	1.93	1.26
Chota	Mr2-18	Historic	Octagonal	0	77	40.60	1.90	1.24
Chota	Mr2-20	Historic	Circular	0	22	29.17	.75	.49
Chota	Mr2-25	Historic	Circular	0	36	38.55	.93	.61
Chota	Mr2-27	Historic	Circular	0	35	35.30	.99	.65
Coweeta Creek	Ma34-3	Mississippian	Square	3	441[c]	40.97	10.76	2.50
Coweeta Creek	Ma34-4	Mississippian	Square	2	339[c]	30.10	11.26	2.61
Coweeta Creek	Ma34-5	Mississippian	Square	5	343[c]	49.15	6.98	1.62
Coweeta Creek	Ma34-6	Mississippian	Square	2	462[c]	37.16	12.43	2.88
Coweeta Creek	Ma34-7	Mississippian	Circular	4	601[c]	61.32	9.80	2.27
Coweeta Creek	Ma34-8	Mississippian	Square	3	266[c]	37.07	7.18	1.66
King	King-4	Mississippian	Square	1	187[c]	29.73	6.29	1.46
Mialoquo	Mr3-1	Historic	Circular	2	48	40.30	1.19	.78
Tanasee	Mr62-3	Historic	Circular	1	80	38.55	2.07	1.36
Tanasee	Mr62-5	Historic	Circular	2	42	38.55	1.09	.71
Toqua	Mr6-2	Mississippian	Square	4	596	85.56	6.97	1.62

Site	Structure	Period	Shape					
Toqua	Mr6-4	Mississippian	Square	4	179	35.30	5.07	1.18
Toqua	Mr6-9	Mississippian	Square	1	116	27.13	4.28	.99
Toqua	Mr6-13	Mississippian	Square	3	131	41.71	3.14	.73
Toqua	Mr6-15	Mississippian	Square	0	244	33.45	7.30	1.69
Toqua	Mr6-18	Mississippian	Square	5	499	36.42	13.70	3.18
Toqua	Mr6-19	Mississippian	Square	1	194	31.77	6.11	1.42
Toqua	Mr6-22	Mississippian	Square	1	176	40.41	4.36	1.01
Toqua	Mr6-23	Mississippian	Square	2	157	39.02	4.02	.93
Toqua	Mr6-24	Mississippian	Square	2	193	47.01	4.11	.95
Toqua	Mr6-30	Mississippian	Square	1	157	49.42	3.18	.74
Toqua	Mr6-33	Mississippian	Square	1	273	53.88	5.07	1.18
Toqua	Mr6-39	Mississippian	Square	6	389	37.16	10.47	2.43
Toqua	Mr6-104	Historic	Circular	1	69	29.17	2.37	1.55
Toqua	Mr6-118	Mississippian	Square	2	193	62.80	3.07	.71
Toqua	Mr6-57	Mississippian	Square	1	73	18.58	3.93	.91
Toqua	Mr6-58	Mississippian	Square	1	75	18.58	4.04	.94
Toqua	Mr6-59	Historic	Circular	1	59	30.66	1.92	1.26
Townsend	Bt89-1	Historic	Circular	1	22	44.31	.50	.32
Townsend	Bt91-8	Historic	Octagonal	1	56	38.08	1.47	.96
Townsend	Bt90-12	Historic	Circular	1	75	44.29	1.69	1.18
Townsend	Bt90-22	Historic	Octagonal	1	54	45.31	1.19	.78
Townsend	Bt90-47	Historic	Octagonal	1	53	36.70	1.44	.94
Tuckaseegee	Jk12-1	Historic	Octagonal	1	30[c]	38.60	.78	.51

[a] The lack of hearths in many structures is due to plow disturbance.

[b] Standardization involved dividing the post density values by the median post density of non-rebuilt houses (the median values are 4.1 for Mississippian houses and 1.53 for Cherokee houses).

[c] These values were determined by the author by counting the posts in published scale drawings.

References Cited

Abler, Thomas S.
1992   Beavers and Muskets: Iroquois Military Fortunes in the Face of European Colonization. In *War in the Tribal Zone: Expanding States and Indigenous Warfare,* edited by R. B. Ferguson and N. L. Whitehead, pp. 151–174. School of American Research Press, Santa Fe, New Mexico.

Adair, James
1986   *A History of the North American Indians.* Promontory Press, New York.
[1775]

Allen, John, Doreen Massey, and Allen Cochrane
1998   *Rethinking the Region.* Routledge, New York.

Allison, Penelope M.
1999   Introduction. In *The Archaeology of Household Activities,* edited by P. M. Allison, pp. 1–18. Routledge, London.

Anderson, Benedict
1991   *Imagined Communities: Reflections on the Origins and Spread of Nationalism.* Verso, London.

Appadurai, Arjun
1997   The Production of Locality. In *Modernity at Large,* pp. 178–200. University of Minnesota Press, Minneapolis.

Ashley, Keith H.
1988   Effects of European and American Colonization of the Southeast on Upper Creek Settlement Patterns: 1700–1800. Unpublished Master's thesis, Department of Anthropology, Florida State University, Tallahassee.

Baden, William W.
1983   *Tomotley: An Eighteenth Century Cherokee Village.* Report of Investigations 36. Department of Anthropology, University of Tennessee, Knoxville.

Barker, Eirlys M.

1993   "Much Blood and Treasure": South Carolina's Indian Traders, 1670–1755. Unpublished Ph.D. dissertation, Department of History, The College of William and Mary, Williamsburg, Virginia.

2001   Indian Traders, Charles Town, and London's Vital Links to the Interior of North America, 1717–1755. In *Money, Trade, and Power: The Evolution of Colonial South Carolina's Plantation Society,* edited by J. P. Greene, R. Brana-Shute, and R. J. Sparks, pp. 141–165. University of South Carolina Press, Columbia.

Barnwell, John

1719   Census of Indians of South Carolina and Nearby, 1715. In *Records in the British Public Record Office Relating to South Carolina, 1663–1717,* vol. 7, pp. 233–239. Microfilm, Charleston County Public Library, Charleston, South Carolina.

Barth, Fredrik

1969   Introduction. In *Ethnic Groups and Boundaries: The Social Organization of Culture Difference,* edited by F. Barth, pp. 9–38. Little and Brown, Boston.

Bartram, William

1996   Travels Through North and South Carolina, Georgia, East and West Florida,
[1791] the Cherokee Country, the Extensive Territories of the Muscogulges or Creek Confederacy, and the Country of the Chactaws. In *Bartram: Travels and Other Writings,* edited by T. P. Slaughter, pp. 3–426. Literary Classics, New York.

Bass, Quentin R.

1977   Prehistoric Settlement and Subsistence Patterns in the Great Smoky Mountains. Unpublished Master's thesis, Department of Anthropology, University of Tennessee, Knoxville.

Bates, James F.

1986   Aboriginal Ceramic Artifacts. In *Overhill Cherokee Archaeology at Chota-Tanasee,* edited by G. F. Schroedl, pp. 289–331. Report of Investigations 38. Department of Anthropology, University of Tennessee, Knoxville.

Bauxar, Joseph J.

1957a Yuchi Ethnoarchaeology. Part I: Some Yuchi Identifications Reconsidered. *Ethnohistory* 4:279–301.

1957b Yuchi Ethnoarchaeology: Parts II–V. *Ethnohistory* 4:369–464.

Baxter, Michael J.

1994   *Exploratory Multivariate Analysis in Archaeology.* Edinburgh University Press, Edinburgh, U.K.

Bech, Jens-Henrik

1988   Correspondence Analysis and Pottery Chronology. In *Multivariate Archaeology: Numerical Approaches in Scandinavian Archaeology,* edited by T. Madsen, pp. 29–35. Aarhus University Press, Aarhus, Denmark.

Beck, Robin A., Jr. (editor)
2007   *The Durable House: House Society Models in Archaeology.* Occasional Paper 35. Center for Archaeological Investigations, Southern Illinois University, Carbondale.

Bentz, Charles, Jr., and Lance Greene
1991   *Archaeological Investigations at the Site 40BT47: A Multicomponent Site in the Eastern Ridge and Valley of East Tennessee.* Draft report submitted to the Tennessee Department of Transportation, Nashville.

Blanton, Richard E.
1994   *Houses and Households: A Comparative Study.* Plenum Press, New York.

Blew, Joseph O., and John W. Kulp
1964   *Service Records on Treated and Untreated Fence Posts.* U.S. Forest Service Research Note FPL-068. Forest Products Laboratory, Forest Service, U.S. Department of Agriculture, Madison, Wisconsin.

Bogan, Arthur E., Lori LaValley, and Gerald F. Schroedl
1986   Faunal Remains. In *Overhill Cherokee Archaeology at Chota-Tanasee,* edited by G. F. Schroedl, pp. 469–514. Report of Investigations 38. Department of Anthropology, University of Tennessee, Knoxville.

Bolstad, Paul V., and Ted L. Gragson
2008   Resource Abundance Constraints on the Early Post-Contact Cherokee Population. *Journal of Archaeological Science* 35:563–576.

Boudreaux, Edmond A.
2007   *The Archaeology of Town Creek.* University of Alabama Press, Tuscaloosa.

Bourdieu, Pierre
1977   *Outline of a Theory of Practice.* Cambridge University Press, New York.

Bowne, Eric E.
2005   *The Westo Indians: Slave Traders of the Early Colonial South.* University of Alabama Press, Tuscaloosa.
2006   "A Bold and Warlike People": The Basis of Westo Power. In *Light on the Path: The Anthropology and History of the Southeastern Indians,* edited by T. J. Pluckhahn and R. Ethridge, pp. 123–132. University of Alabama Press, Tuscaloosa.

Boyd, Robert, and Peter J. Richerson
1987   The Evolution of Ethnic Markers. *Cultural Anthropology* 2:65–79.

Brain, Jeffrey P.
1979   *Tunica Treasure.* Papers of the Peabody Museum of Archaeology and Ethnology 71. Harvard University, Cambridge, Massachusetts.

Braun, E. Lucy
1950   *Deciduous Forests of Eastern North America.* Blakiston Company, Garden City, New Jersey.

Braund, Kathryn E.
1993   *Deerskins and Duffels: The Creek Indian Trade with Anglo-America, 1686–1815.* University of Nebraska Press, Lincoln.

Briceland, Alan V.
1987   *Westward from Virginia: The Exploration of the Virginia-Carolina Frontier, 1650–1710.* University Press of Virginia, Charlottesville.

Bushnell, Amy T.
1994   *Situado and Sabana: Spain's Support System for the Presidio and Mission Provinces of Florida.* Anthropological Papers 74. American Museum of Natural History, New York.

Bushnell, David I., Jr.
1907   Discoveries Beyond the Appalachian Mountains in September, 1671. *American Anthropologist* 9:45–56.

Cable, John S., and Mary B. Reed
2000   Archaeological Excavations in Brasstown Valley: Qualla/Lamar Occupations. *Early Georgia* 28(2):112–143.

Callon, Michele
1986   Some Elements of a Sociology of Translation: Domestication of the Scallops and the Fishermen of Saint Brieuc Bay. In *Power, Action and Belief: A New Sociology of Knowledge?* edited by J. Law, pp. 196–233. Routledge and Kegan Paul, London.

Casselberry, Samuel E.
1974   Further Refinement of Formulae for Determining Population from Floor Area. *World Archaeology* 6:117–122.

Chapman, Jefferson (editor)
1979   *The 1978 Archaeological Investigations at the Citico Site (40Mr7).* Report submitted to the Tennessee Valley Authority, Knoxville.

Chicken, George
1894   Journal of the March of the Carolinians into the Cherokee Mountains, in
[1715] the Yemassee Indian War, 1715–1716. In *Year Book, 1894,* edited by L. Cheves, pp. 313–354. City of Charleston, South Carolina.
1916   Journal of the Commissioner for Indian Affairs on His Journey to the
[1725] Cherokees and His Proceedings There. In *Travels in the American Colonies,* edited by N. D. Mereness, pp. 95–174. MacMillan, New York.

Chilton, Elizabeth S.
1999   Meaningful Materials and Material Meanings: An Introduction. In *Material Meanings: Critical Approaches to the Interpretation of Material Culture,* edited by E. S. Chilton, pp. 1–6. University of Utah Press, Salt Lake City.

Clowse, Converse D.
1971   *Economic Beginnings in Colonial South Carolina, 1670–1730.* University of South Carolina Press, Columbia.

Coe, Joffrey L.
1961   Cherokee Archaeology. In *The Symposium on Cherokee and Iroquois Culture,* edited by W. N. Fenton and J. Gulick, pp. 51–61. Bureau of American Ethnology Bulletin 180. Smithsonian Institution Press, Washington, D.C.

Conkey, Margaret W.
1999   An End Note: Reframing Materiality for Archaeology. In *Material Mean-*

ings: Critical Approaches to the Interpretation of Material Culture, edited by E. S. Chilton, pp. 133–141. University of Utah Press, Salt Lake City.

Cook, Robert A.

2007   Single Component Sites with Long Sequences of Radiocarbon Dates: The Sunwatch Site and Middle Fort Ancient Village Growth. *American Antiquity* 72:439–460.

Cook, Sherburne F.

1972   *Prehistoric Demography.* McCaleb Module in Anthropology 16. Addison-Wesley, Reading, Massachusetts.

Corkran, David H.

1962   *The Cherokee Frontier, 1740–1762.* University of Oklahoma Press, Norman.

1967   *The Creek Frontier, 1540–1783.* University of Oklahoma Press, Norman.

Crane, Verner W.

1916   The Tennessee River as the Road to Carolina: The Beginnings of Exploration and Trade. *The Mississippi Valley Historical Review* 3(1):3–18.

2004   *The Southern Frontier, 1670–1732.* University of Alabama Press, Tuscaloosa. Originally published 1929, Duke University Press, Durham, North Carolina.

Crosby, Alfred W., Jr.

1972   *The Columbian Exchange.* Greenwood Press, Westport, Connecticut.

Cumming, William P.

1998   *The Southeast in Early Maps.* 3rd ed., revised and enlarged by L. DeVorsey Jr. University of North Carolina Press, Chapel Hill.

Davis, R. P. Stephen, Jr.

2002   The Cultural Landscape of the North Carolina Piedmont at Contact. In *The Transformation of the Southeastern Indians, 1540–1760,* edited by R. Ethridge and C. Hudson, pp. 135–154. University Press of Mississippi, Jackson.

DeBoer, Warren R.

1988   Subterranean Storage and the Organization of Surplus: The View from Eastern North America. *Southeastern Archaeology* 7:1–20.

DePratter, Chester B., and Stanley A. South

1990   *Charlesfort: The 1989 Search Project.* Research Manuscript Series 210. South Carolina Institute of Archaeology and Anthropology, Columbia.

Dickens, Roy S., Jr.

1976   *Cherokee Prehistory: The Pisgah Phase in the Appalachian Summit.* University of Tennessee Press, Knoxville.

1979   The Origins and Development of Cherokee Culture. In *The Cherokee Indian Nation: A Troubled History,* edited by D. H. King, pp. 3–32. University of Tennessee Press, Knoxville.

1985   The Form, Function, and Formation of Garbage-Filled Pits on Southeastern Aboriginal Sites: An Archaeobotanical Analysis. In *Structure and Process in Southeastern Archaeology,* edited by R. S. Dickens Jr. and H. T. Ward, pp. 34–59. University of Alabama Press, Tuscaloosa.

1986   An Evolutionary-Ecological Interpretation of Cherokee Cultural Development. In *The Conference on Cherokee Prehistory,* compiled by D. G. Moore, pp. 81–94. Warren Wilson College, Swannanoa, North Carolina.

Dietler, Michael, and Ingrid Herbich
1998   Habitus, Techniques, Style: An Integrated Approach to the Social Understanding of Material Culture and Boundaries. In *The Archaeology of Social Boundaries,* edited by M. T. Stark, pp. 232–263. Smithsonian Institution Press, Washington, D.C.

Dobres, Marcia-Anne A.
1999   Technology's Links and Chaines: The Processual Unfolding of Technique and Technician. In *The Social Dynamics of Technology: Practice, Politics, and World Views,* edited by M. A. Dobres and C. Hoffman, pp. 124–146. Smithsonian Institution Press, Washington, D.C.
2000   *Technology and Social Agency.* Blackwell, Oxford.

Dobyns, Henry F.
1983   *Their Number Become Thinned: Native American Population Dynamics in Eastern North America.* University of Tennessee Press, Knoxville.

Drooker, Penelope B.
2002   The Ohio Valley, 1550–1750: Patterns of Sociopolitical Coalescence and Dispersal. In *The Transformation of the Southeastern Indians, 1540–1760,* edited by R. Ethridge and C. Hudson, pp. 115–134. University Press of Mississippi, Jackson.

Duff, Andrew I.
1996   Ceramic Micro-Seriation: Types or Attributes? *American Antiquity* 61:89–101.

Duff, Meaghan N.
2001   Creating a Plantation Province: Proprietary Land Policies and Early Settlement Patterns. In *Money, Trade, and Power: The Evolution of Colonial South Carolina's Plantation Society,* edited by J. P. Greene, R. Brana-Shute, and R. J. Sparks, pp. 1–25. University of South Carolina Press, Columbia.

Duncan, Barbara R., and Brett H. Riggs
2003   *Cherokee Heritage Trails Guidebook.* University of North Carolina Press, Chapel Hill.

Dye, David H.
2002   Warfare in the Protohistoric Southeast: 1500–1700. In *Between Contacts and Colonies: Archaeological Perspectives on the Protohistoric Southeast,* edited by C. B. Wesson and M. A. Rees, pp. 126–141. University of Alabama Press, Tuscaloosa.

Egloff, Brian J.
1967   An Analysis of Ceramics from Historic Cherokee Towns. Unpublished Master's thesis, Department of Anthropology, University of North Carolina, Chapel Hill.

Esarey, Duane
2007   The 17th-Century Midwestern Slave Trade in Colonial Context. Paper presented at the 2007 Midwest Archaeological Conference, South Bend, Indiana.

Ethridge, Robbie
2006   Creating the Shatter Zone: Indian Slave Traders and the Collapse of the Southeastern Chiefdoms. In *Light on the Path: The Anthropology and History of the Southeastern Indians,* edited by T. J. Pluckhahn and R. Ethridge, pp. 207–218. University of Alabama Press, Tuscaloosa.

Eveleigh, Samuel
1715   Letter to John Boone and Richard Berresford, July 19, 1715. In *Records in the British Public Record Office Relating to South Carolina, 1663–1717,* vol. 6, pp. 103–104. Microfilm, Charleston County Public Library, Charleston, South Carolina.

Ferguson, R. Brian, and Neil L. Whitehead
1992   The Violent Edge of Empire. In *War in the Tribal Zone: Expanding States and Indigenous Warfare,* edited by R. B. Ferguson and N. L. Whitehead, pp. 1–30. School of American Research Press, Santa Fe, New Mexico.

Fleming, Victor K.
1976   Historic Aboriginal Occupation of the Guntersville Basin, Alabama. Unpublished Master's thesis, Department of Anthropology, University of Alabama, Tuscaloosa.

Franklin, W. Neil
1932   Virginia and the Cherokee Indian Trade, 1673–1752. *East Tennessee Historical Society's Publications* 4:3–21. Knoxville.

Gallay, Alan
2002   *The Indian Slave Trade: The Rise of the English Empire in the American South, 1670–1717.* Yale University Press, New Haven, Connecticut.

Galloway, Patricia K.
1995   *Choctaw Genesis, 1500–1700.* University of Nebraska Press, Lincoln.
2002   Colonial Period Transformations in the Mississippi Valley: Disintegration, Alliance, Confederation, Playoff. In *The Transformation of the Southeastern Indians, 1540–1760,* edited by R. Ethridge and C. Hudson, pp. 225–248. University Press of Mississippi, Jackson.

Gearing, Fred
1962   *Priests and Warriors: Structures for Cherokee Politics in the Eighteenth Century.* Memoir 93. American Anthropological Association, Washington, D.C.

Giddens, Anthony
1979   *Central Problems in Social Theory.* MacMillan, London.

Gilbert, William H., Jr.
1943   *The Eastern Cherokee.* Bureau of American Ethnology Bulletin 133. Smithsonian Institution, Washington, D.C.

Greene, Jack P.
1989   Early South Carolina and the Psychology of British Colonization. In *Selling a New World: Two Colonial South Carolina Promotional Pamphlets,* edited by J. P. Greene, pp. 1–32. University of South Carolina Press, Columbia.

Guthe, Alfred K., and Marian Bistline
1981   *Excavations at Tomotley, 1973–74, and the Tuskegee Area: Two Reports.* Re-

port of Investigations 24. Department of Anthropology, University of Tennessee, Knoxville.

Haan, Richard L.

1981   The "Trade Do's Not Flourish as Formerly": The Ecological Origins of the Yamassee War of 1715. *Ethnohistory* 28:341–358.

Hally, David J.

1986a   The Cherokee Archaeology of Georgia. In *The Conference on Cherokee Prehistory,* compiled by D. G. Moore, pp. 95–121. Warren Wilson College, Swannanoa, North Carolina.

1986b   The Identification of Vessel Function: A Case Study from Northwest Georgia. *American Antiquity* 51:267–295.

1988   Archaeology and Settlement Plan of the King Site. In *The King Site: Continuity and Contact in Sixteenth-Century Georgia,* edited by R. L. Blakely, pp. 3–16. University of Georgia Press, Athens.

1994   An Overview of Lamar Archaeology. In *Ocmulgee Archaeology, 1936–1986,* edited by D. J. Hally, pp. 144–174. University of Georgia Press, Athens.

2002   As Caves Beneath the Ground: Making Sense of Aboriginal House Form in the Protohistoric and Historic Southeast. In *Between Contacts and Colonies: Archaeological Perspectives on the Protohistoric Southeast,* edited by C. B. Wesson and M. A. Rees, pp. 90–109. University of Alabama Press, Tuscaloosa.

Hally, David J., and Hypatia Kelly

1998   The Nature of Mississippian Towns in Georgia: The King Site Example. In *Mississippian Towns and Sacred Spaces: Searching for an Architectural Grammar,* edited by R. B. Lewis and C. Stout, pp. 49–63. University of Alabama Press, Tuscaloosa.

Harmon, Michael A.

1986   *Eighteenth-Century Lower Cherokee Adaptation and Use of European Material Culture.* Volumes in Historical Archaeology 2. South Carolina Institute of Archaeology and Anthropology, Columbia.

Hassan, Fekri A.

1981   *Demographic Archaeology.* Academic Press, New York.

Hatch, James W.

1995   Lamar Period Upland Farmsteads of the Oconee River Valley, Georgia. In *Mississippian Communities and Households,* edited by J. D. Rogers and B. D. Smith, pp. 135–155. University of Alabama Press, Tuscaloosa.

Hatley, M. Thomas

1995   *The Dividing Paths: Cherokees and South Carolinians Through the Era of Revolution.* Oxford University Press, Oxford.

Hegmon, Michelle

1998   Technology, Style, and Social Practices: Archaeological Approaches. In *The Archaeology of Social Boundaries,* edited by M. T. Stark, pp. 264–280. Smithsonian Institution Press, Washington, D.C.

Heye, George G.
1919   *Certain Mounds in Haywood County, North Carolina.* Contributions from the Museum of the American Indian 5(3), pp. 35–43. Heye Foundation, New York.

Heye, George G., Frederick W. Hodge, and George H. Pepper
1918   *The Nacoochee Mound in Georgia.* Contributions from the Museum of the American Indian 4(3), pp. 1–103. Heye Foundation, New York.

Hicks, Charles
1826   Letter to John Ross, February 1, 1826. In *Traditions and History of the Cherokee Indians to 1776,* vol. 7, by J. H. Payne, pp. 1–4. Unpublished manuscript on microfilm, Davis Library, University of North Carolina, Chapel Hill.

Hodder, Ian, and Craig Cessford
2004   Daily Practice and Social Memory at Catalhoyuk. *American Antiquity* 69:17–41.

Howard, A. Eric
1997   *An Intrasite Spatial Analysis of Surface Collections at Chattooga: A Lower Town Cherokee Village.* Report submitted to the U.S. Forest Service, Francis Marion and Sumter National Forests, South Carolina.

Howell, Cameron
2005   Overhill Pottery from the Townsend Site. Paper presented at the Cherokee Ceramics Workshop, Research Laboratories of Archaeology, University of North Carolina, Chapel Hill.

Hudson, Charles
2002   Introduction. In *The Transformation of the Southeastern Indians, 1540–1760,* edited by R. Ethridge and C. Hudson, pp. xi–xxxix. University Press of Mississippi, Jackson.

Hughes, Pryce
1713   Letter to the Dutchess of Ormond, October 15, 1713. In *Five Pryce Hughes Autograph Letters, Proposing a Welsh Colony.* South Caroliniana Library, University of South Carolina, Columbia.

Jeter, Marvin D.
2002   From Prehistory Through Protohistory to Ethnohistory in and near the Northern Lower Mississippi Valley. In *The Transformation of the Southeastern Indians, 1540–1760,* edited by R. Ethridge and C. Hudson, pp. 177–223. University Press of Mississippi, Jackson.

Johnson, Nathaniel, Thomas Broughton, Robert Gibbs, George Smith, and Richard Beresford
1708   Census. In *Records in the British Public Record Office Relating to South Carolina, 1663–1717,* vol. 2, pp. 203–209. Microfilm, Charleston County Public Library, Charleston, South Carolina.

Joyce, Rosemary A., and Julia A. Hendon
2000   Heterarchy, History, and Material Reality: "Communities" in Late Classic Honduras. In *The Archaeology of Communities: A New World Perspective,* edited by M. A. Canuto and J. Yaeger, pp. 143–160. Routledge, New York.

Keel, Bennie C.
1976   *Cherokee Archaeology: A Study of the Appalachian Summit.* University of Tennessee Press, Knoxville.

Kelly, Arthur R., and Clemens de Baillou
1960   Excavations of the Presumptive Site of Estatoe. *Southern Indian Studies* 12:3–30.

Kelly, Arthur R., and Robert S. Neitzel
1961   *The Chauga Site in Oconee County, South Carolina.* Laboratory of Archaeology Report 3. University of Georgia, Athens.

Kelton, Paul
2002   The Great Southeastern Smallpox Epidemic, 1696–1700: The Region's First Major Epidemic. In *The Transformation of the Southeastern Indians, 1540–1760,* edited by R. Ethridge and C. Hudson, pp. 21–37. University Press of Mississippi, Jackson.

King, Duane H.
1977   Vessel Morphology and Eighteenth-Century Overhill Ceramics. *Journal of Cherokee Studies* 2:154–169.

Klinck, Carl F.
1970   Biographical Introduction. In *The Journal of Major John Norton, 1816,* edited by C. F. Klinck and J. J. Talman, pp. xiii–xcviii. The Champlain Society, Toronto.

Knight, Vernon James, Jr.
1994   The Formation of the Creeks. In *The Forgotten Centuries: Indians and Europeans in the American South, 1521–1704,* edited by C. Hudson and C. C. Tesser, pp. 373–392. University of Georgia Press, Athens.

Koldehoff, Brad, and Joseph M. Galloy
2006   Late Woodland Frontiers in the American Bottom Region. *Southeastern Archaeology* 25:275–300.

Kowalewski, Stephen A.
2006   Coalescent Societies. In *Light on the Path: The Anthropology and History of the Southeastern Indians,* edited by T. J. Pluckhahn and R. Ethridge, pp. 94–122. University of Alabama Press, Tuscaloosa.

Krzyzewski, J. C., C. Ralph, and B. Spicer
1980   *Performance of Preservative-Treated Fence Posts After 43 Years of Tests.* Eastern Forest Products Laboratory, Environment Canada. Report submitted to Forintek Canada Corp., Ottawa.

Latour, Bruno
1991   Technology Is Society Made Durable. In *A Sociology of Monsters: Essays on Power, Technology and Domination,* edited by J. Law, pp. 103–131. Routledge, London.
1992   Where Are the Missing Masses? Sociology of a Few Mundane Artifacts. In *Shaping Technology, Building Society: Studies in Sociotechnical Change,* edited by W. Bijker and J. Law, pp. 225–258. MIT Press, Cambridge, Massachusetts.

1999   On Recalling ANT. In *Actor Network Theory and After,* edited by J. Law and J. Hassard, pp. 15–25. Blackwell, Oxford.

2005   *Reassembling the Social: An Introduction to Actor-Network-Theory.* Oxford University Press, Oxford.

Law, John

1999   After ANT: Topology, Naming and Complexity. In *Actor Network Theory and After,* edited by J. Law and J. Hassard, pp. 1–14. Blackwell, Oxford.

Law, Robin

1992   Warfare on the West African Slave Coast, 1650–1850. In *War in the Tribal Zone: Expanding States and Indigenous Warfare,* edited by R. B. Ferguson and N. L. Whitehead, pp. 103–126. School of American Research Press, Santa Fe, New Mexico.

Lee, Wayne E.

2004   Fortify, Fight, or Flee: Tuscarora and Cherokee Defensive Warfare and Military Culture Adaptation. *The Journal of Military History* 68:713–770.

Lefebvre, Henri

1991   *The Production of Space.* Basil Blackwell, Oxford.

Le Jau, Francis

1956a   Letter to the Secretary, April 22, 1708. In *The Carolina Chronicle of Dr.*

[1708]   *Francis Le Jau, 1706–1717,* edited by F. J. Klingberg, pp. 37–41. University of California Publications in History 53. University of California Press, Berkeley.

1956b   Letter to the Secretary, August 10, 1713. In *The Carolina Chronicle of Dr.*

[1713]   *Francis Le Jau, 1706–1717,* edited by F. J. Klingberg, pp. 132–135. University of California Publications in History 53. University of California Press, Berkeley.

1956c   Letter to the Secretary, May 10, 1715. In *The Carolina Chronicle of Dr.*

[1715]   *Francis Le Jau, 1706–1717,* edited by F. J. Klingberg, pp. 151–154. University of California Publications in History 53. University of California Press, Berkeley.

1956d   Letter to the Secretary, May 21, 1715. In *The Carolina Chronicle of Dr.*

[1715]   *Francis Le Jau, 1706–1717,* edited by F. J. Klingberg, pp. 157–160. University of California Publications in History 53. University of California Press, Berkeley.

1956e   Letter to the Secretary, November 28, 1715. In *The Carolina Chronicle of*

[1715]   *Dr. Francis Le Jau, 1706–1717,* edited by F. J. Klingberg, pp. 169–171. University of California Publications in History 53. University of California Press, Berkeley.

Lemonnier, Pierre

1993   Introduction. In *Technological Choices: Transformation in Material Cultures since the Neolithic,* edited by P. Lemonnier, pp. 1–35. Routledge, London.

Lengyel, Stacey N.

2004   Archaeomagnetic Research in the U.S. Midcontinent. Unpublished Ph.D. dissertation, Department of Anthropology, University of Arizona, Tucson.

Lewis, Thomas M. N., and Madeline D. Kneberg
1946   *Hiwassee Island: An Archaeological Account of Four Tennessee Indian Peoples.* University of Tennessee Press, Knoxville.

Lewis, Thomas M. N., Madeline D. Kneberg, and Lynne P. Sullivan
1995   *The Prehistory of the Chickamauga Basin.* University of Tennessee Press, Knoxville.

Lightfoot, Kent G.
2005   *Indians, Missionaries, and Merchants: The Legacy of Colonial Encounters on the California Frontiers.* University of California Press, Berkeley.

Lightfoot, Kent G., Antoinette Martinez, and Ann M. Schiff
1998   Daily Practice and Material Culture in Pluralistic Social Settings: An Archaeological Study of Culture Change and Persistence from Fort Ross, California. *American Antiquity* 63:199–222.

Lincoln, Bruce
1989   *Discourse and the Construction of Society: Comparative Studies of Myth, Ritual, and Classification.* Oxford University Press, New York.

Long, Alexander
1969   A Small Postscript on the ways and maners of the Indians called Cheri-
[1725]   kees. *Southeastern Indian Studies* 21:5–49.

Low, Setha M., and Denise Lawrence Zúñiga
2003   Locating Culture. In *The Anthropology of Space and Place: Locating Culture,* edited by S. M. Low and D. Zúñiga, pp. 1–48. Blackwell, Oxford.

Lyman, R. Lee, Michael J. O'Brien, and Robert C. Dunnell
1997   *The Rise and Fall of Culture History.* Plenum Press, New York.

McDowell, William L., Jr. (editor)
1992   *Journals of the Commissioners of the Indian Trade, September 20, 1710–August 29, 1718.* South Carolina Department of Archives and History, Columbia.

McEwan, Bonnie G. (editor)
1993   *The Spanish Missions of La Florida.* University Press of Florida, Gainesville.

McGill, Robert, John W. Tukey, and Wayne A. Larsen
1978   Variations of Box Plots. *The American Statistician* 32:12–16.

McIntosh, Roderick J.
1974   Archaeology and Mud Wall Decay in a West African Village. *World Archaeology* 6:154–171.

McKern, William C.
1939   The Midwestern Taxonomic Method as an Aid to Archaeological Culture Study. *American Antiquity* 4:301–313.
1943   Regarding Midwestern Archaeological Taxonomy. *American Anthropologist* 45:313–315.

MacLean, J. D.
1926   Service Tests on Treated and Untreated Fence Posts. *Proceedings of the American Wood-Preservers' Association,* pp. 401–423.

Madsen, Torsten
1988   Multivariate Statistics and Archaeology. In *Multivariate Archaeology: Numerical Approaches in Scandinavian Archaeology,* edited by T. Madsen, pp. 7–27. Aarhus University Press, Aarhus, Denmark.

Malone, Patrick M.
1991   *The Skulking Way of War: Technology and Tactics among the New England Indians.* Madison Press, Toronto.

Marcoux, Jon Bernard
2008   Cherokee Households and Communities in the English Contact Period, A.D. 1670–1740. Unpublished Ph.D. dissertation, Department of Anthropology, University of North Carolina, Chapel Hill.

Martin, Joel W.
1994   Southeastern Indians and the English Trade in Skins and Slaves. In *The Forgotten Centuries: Indians and Europeans in the American South, 1521–1704,* edited by C. Hudson and C. C. Tesser, pp. 304–324. University of Georgia Press, Athens.

Matthew, A. J., A. J. Woods, and C. Oliver
1997   Spots Before the Eyes: New Comparison Charts for Visual Percentage Estimation in Archaeological Material. In *Recent Developments in Ceramic Petrology,* edited by A. Middleton and I. Freestone, pp. 211–263. Occasional Paper 81. British Museum, London.

Merrell, John H.
1989a   *The Indians' New World: Catawbas and Their Neighbors from European Contact Through the Era of Removal.* University of North Carolina Press, Chapel Hill.
1989b   "Our Bond of Peace": Patterns of Intercultural Exchange in the Carolina Piedmont, 1650–1750. In *Powhatan's Mantle: Indians in the Colonial Southeast,* edited by P. H. Wood, G. A. Waselkov, and M. T. Hatley, pp. 196–222. University of Nebraska Press, Lincoln.

Milner, George R.
1980   Epidemic Disease in the Postcontact Southeast: A Reappraisal. *Midcontinental Journal of Archaeology* 5:39–56.

Mooney, James
1889   Cherokee Mound Building. *American Anthropologist* 2:167–171.
1900   *Myths of the Cherokee.* Bureau of American Ethnology Annual Report 19, pp. 1–576. Smithsonian Institution, Washington, D.C.

Moore, Alexander
1988   Introduction. In *Nairne's Muskhogean Journals: The 1708 Expedition to the Mississippi River,* edited by A. Moore, pp. 1–31. University Press of Mississippi, Jackson.

Moore, Jerry D., and Janine Gasco
1990   Perishable Structures and Serial Dwellings from Coastal Chiapas. *Ancient Mesoamerica* 1:205–212.

Muller, John
1997   *Mississippian Political Economy.* Plenum Press, New York.
Myer, William E.
1928   *Indian Trails of the Southeast.* Bureau of American Ethnology Annual Report 42. Smithsonian Institution, Washington, D.C.
Nairne, Thomas
1988   Thomas Nairne's Memorial to Charles Spencer, Earl of Sunderland. In
[1708] *Nairne's Muskhogean Journals: The 1708 Expedition to the Mississippi River,* edited by A. Moore, pp. 73–79. University Press of Mississippi, Jackson.
1989   A Letter from South Carolina. In *Selling a New World: Two Colonial South*
[1710] *Carolina Promotional Pamphlets,* edited by J. P. Greene, pp. 33–76. University of South Carolina Press, Columbia.
Nash, R. C.
2001   The Organization of Trade and Finance in the Atlantic Economy: Britain and South Carolina, 1670–1775. In *Money, Trade, and Power: The Evolution of Colonial South Carolina's Plantation Society,* edited by J. P. Greene, R. Brana-Shute, and R. J. Sparks, pp. 74–107. University of South Carolina Press, Columbia.
Newman, Robert D.
1986   Euro-American Artifacts. In *Overhill Cherokee Archaeology at Chota-Tanasee,* edited by G. F. Schroedl, pp. 415–468. Report of Investigations 38. Department of Anthropology, University of Tennessee, Knoxville.
Norris, John
1989   Profitable Advice for Rich and Poor. In *Selling a New World: Two Colonial*
[1712] *South Carolina Promotional Pamphlets,* edited by J. P. Greene, pp. 77–147. University of South Carolina Press, Columbia.
Norton, John
1970   Journal. In *The Journal of Major John Norton, 1816,* edited by C. F. Klinck
[1816] and J. J. Talman, pp. 1–370. The Champlain Society, Toronto.
Norval, Aletta J.
1996   Thinking Identities: Against a Theory of Ethnicity. In *The Politics of Difference: Ethnic Premises in a World of Power,* edited by E. N. Wilmsen and P. McAllister, pp. 59–70. University of Chicago Press, Chicago.
Oatis, Steven J.
2004   *A Colonial Complex: South Carolina's Frontiers in the Era of the Yamasee War, 1680–1730.* University of Nebraska Press, Lincoln.
Orton, Clive, Paul Tyers, and Alan Vince
1993   *Pottery in Archaeology.* Cambridge University Press, Cambridge.
Pauketat, Timothy R.
1989   Monitoring Mississippian Homestead Occupation Span and Economy Using Ceramic Refuse. *American Antiquity* 54:288–310.
2000a   Politicization and Community in the Pre-Columbian Mississippi Valley. In *The Archaeology of Communities: A New World Perspective,* edited by M. A. Canuto and J. Yaeger, pp. 16–43. Routledge, New York.

2000b   The Tragedy of the Commoners. In *Agency in Archaeology,* edited by M. A. Dobres and J. E. Robb, pp. 113–129. Routledge, London.

2001   A New Tradition in Archaeology. In *The Archaeology of Traditions: Agency and History Before and After Columbus,* edited by T. R. Pauketat, pp. 1–16. University Press of Florida, Gainesville.

2003   Resettled Farmers and the Making of a Mississippian Polity. *American Antiquity* 68:39–66.

Payne, John H.
1814–   *Traditions and History of the Cherokee Indians to 1776,* vol. 3. Unpublished
1841   manuscript on microfilm, Davis Library, University of North Carolina, Chapel Hill.

Pennington, Edgar L.
1931   The South Carolina Indian War of 1715, as Seen by the Clergymen. *South Carolina Historical and Genealogical Magazine* 32(4):251–269.

Perdue, Theda
1998   *Cherokee Women: Gender and Culture Change, 1700–1835.* University of Nebraska Press, Lincoln.

Perttula, Timothy K.
2002   Social Changes among the Caddo Indians in the Sixteenth and Seventeenth Centuries. In *The Transformation of the Southeastern Indians, 1540–1760,* edited by R. Ethridge and C. Hudson, pp. 249–270. University Press of Mississippi, Jackson.

Polhemus, Richard (editor)
1987   *The Toqua Site: A Late Mississippian Dallas Phase Town.* Report of Investigations 41. Department of Anthropology, University of Tennessee, Knoxville.

Purslow, D. F.
1976   *Results of Field Tests on the Natural Durability of Timber (1932–1975).* Building Research Establishment Current Paper 6/76. Department of the Environment, London.

Ramsey, James G. M.
1999   *The Annals of Tennessee to the End of the Eighteenth Century.* Overmountain
[1853]   Press, Johnson City, Tennessee.

Ramsey, William L.
2001   "All & Singular the Slaves": A Demographic Profile of Slavery in Colonial South Carolina. In *Money, Trade, and Power: The Evolution of Colonial South Carolina's Plantation Society,* edited by J. P. Greene, R. Brana-Shute, and R. J. Sparks, pp. 166–186. University of South Carolina Press, Columbia.

2003   "Something Cloudy in Their Looks": The Origins of the Yamasee War Reconsidered. *The Journal of American History* 90:44–75.

Reid, John P.
1976   *A Better Kind of Hatchet: Law, Trade, and Diplomacy in the Cherokee Nation during the Early Years of European Contact.* Pennsylvania State University Press, University Park.

Riggs, Brett H.
1989   Ethnohistorical and Archaeological Dimensions of Early Nineteenth-Century Cherokee Intrahousehold Variation. In *Households and Communities,* edited by S. MacEachern, D. Archer, and R. Garvin, pp. 328–338. Proceedings of the Chacmool Conference 21. Archaeological Association of the University of Calgary, Calgary, Canada.
1999   Removal Period Cherokee Households in Southwestern North Carolina: Material Perspectives on Ethnicity and Cultural Differentiation. Unpublished Ph.D. dissertation, Department of Anthropology, University of Tennessee, Knoxville.
2010   Chestowee Reconsidered. In *"One of the Other Nations": Yuchi Indian Histories Before the Removal Era,* edited by J. B. Jackson. University of Nebraska Press, Lincoln.

Riggs, Brett H., and Christopher B. Rodning
2002   Cherokee Ceramic Traditions of Southwestern North Carolina. *North Carolina Archaeology* 51:34–54.

Riggs, Brett H., M. Scott Shumate, and Patti Evans-Shumate
1997   *Archaeological Data Recovery at Site 31JK291, Jackson County, North Carolina.* Report submitted to the Eastern Band of Cherokee Indians, Office of Cultural Resources, Cherokee, North Carolina.

Rodd, Charles
1928   Letter to a Gentleman, May 8, 1715. In *Calendar of State Papers, Colonial*
[1715]   *Series, America and West Indies, August 1714–December 1715,* vol. 28, edited by C. Headlam, pp. 166–169. Public Record Office, London.

Rodning, Christopher B.
2002   Reconstructing the Coalescence of Cherokee Communities in Southern Appalachia. In *The Transformation of the Southeastern Indians, 1540–1760,* edited by R. Ethridge and C. Hudson, pp. 155–176. University Press of Mississippi, Jackson.
2004   The Cherokee Town at Coweeta Creek. Unpublished Ph.D. dissertation, Department of Anthropology, University of North Carolina, Chapel Hill.
2007   Building and Rebuilding Cherokee Houses and Townhouses in Southwestern North Carolina. In *The Durable House: House Society Models in Archaeology,* edited by R. A. Beck Jr., pp. 464–484. Occasional Paper 35. Center for Archaeological Investigations, Southern Illinois University, Carbondale.
2009   Mounds, Myths, and Cherokee Townhouses in Southwestern North Carolina. *American Antiquity* 74:627–663.

Romenofsky, Ann F.
1987   *Vectors of Death.* University of New Mexico Press, Albuquerque.

Roosens, Eugene E.
1989   *Creating Ethnicity: The Process of Ethnogenesis.* Sage, London.

Rothrock, Mary U.
1929   Carolina Traders among the Overhill Cherokees, 1690–1760. *East Tennessee Historical Society's Publications* 1:3–18. Knoxville.

Rountree, Helen C.
2002   Trouble Coming Southward: Emanations Through and from Virginia, 1607–
        1675. In *The Transformation of the Southeastern Indians, 1540–1760,* ed-
        ited by R. Ethridge and C. Hudson, pp. 65–78. University Press of Mis-
        sissippi, Jackson.

Russ, Kurt C., and Jefferson Chapman
1983   *Archaeological Investigations at the Eighteenth Century Overhill Cherokee
        Town of Mialoquo.* Report of Investigations 37. Department of Anthropology,
        University of Tennessee, Knoxville.

Salamone, Frank A., and Charles H. Swanson
1979   Identity and Ethnicity: Ethnic Groups and Interactions in a Multi-ethnic
        Society. *Ethnic Groups* 2:167–183.

Scarry, John F.
1995   Apalachee Homesteads: The Basal Social and Economic Units of a Missis-
        sippian Chiefdom. In *Mississippian Communities and Households,* edited by
        J. D. Rogers and B. D. Smith, pp. 201–223. University of Alabama Press,
        Tuscaloosa.

Schroedl, Gerald F.
1986   Toward an Explanation of Cherokee Origins in East Tennessee. In *The
        Conference on Cherokee Prehistory,* compiled by D. G. Moore, pp. 122–138.
        Warren Wilson College, Swannanoa, North Carolina.
1989   Overhill Cherokee Household and Village Patterns in the Eighteenth Cen-
        tury. In *Households and Communities,* edited by S. MacEachern, D. Ar-
        cher, and R. Garvin, pp. 350–360. Proceedings of the Chacmool Confer-
        ence 21. Archaeological Association of the University of Calgary, Calgary,
        Canada.
1994   *A Summary of Archaeological Studies Conducted at the Chattooga Site,
        Oconee County, South Carolina.* Report submitted to the U.S. Forest Ser-
        vice, Francis Marion and Sumter National Forests, South Carolina.
2000   Cherokee Ethnohistory and Archaeology from 1540 to 1838. In *Indians of
        the Greater Southeast: Historical Archaeology and Ethnohistory,* edited by B.
        G. McEwan, pp. 204–241. University Press of Florida, Gainesville.

Schroedl, Gerald F. (editor)
1986   *Overhill Cherokee Archaeology at Chota-Tanasee.* Report of Investigations
        38. Department of Anthropology, University of Tennessee, Knoxville.

Setzler, Frank M., and Jesse D. Jennings
1941   *Peachtree Mound and Village Site, Cherokee County, North Carolina.* Bu-
        reau of American Ethnology Bulletin 131. Smithsonian Institution, Wash-
        ington, D.C.

Shapiro, Gary
1984   Ceramic Vessels, Site Permanence, and Group Size: A Mississippian Ex-
        ample. *American Antiquity* 49:696–712.

Shennan, Stephen
1997   *Quantifying Archaeology.* 2nd ed. University of Iowa Press, Iowa City.

Shumate, M. Scott, Brett H. Riggs, and Larry R. Kimball

2005   *The Alarka Farmstead Site: The Archaeology of a Mid-Seventeenth-Century Cherokee Winter House/Summer House Complex, Swain County, North Carolina.* Report submitted to National Forests in North Carolina, Appalachian State University Laboratories of Archaeological Science, Boone.

Sinclair, Anthony

2000   Constellations of Knowledge: Human Agency and Material Affordance in Lithic Technology. In *Agency in Archaeology,* edited by M. A. Dobres and J. E. Robb, pp. 196–212. Routledge, London.

Skowronek, Russell K.

1991   *Return to Peachtree: A Catalogue of Amateur Surface Collections from Cherokee and Clay Counties, North Carolina.* Report submitted to the North Carolina Department of Cultural Resources, Raleigh.

Smith, Betty A.

1979   Distribution of Eighteenth-Century Cherokee Settlements. In *The Cherokee Indian Nation: A Troubled History,* edited by D. H. King, pp. 46–60. University of Tennessee Press, Knoxville.

Smith, Bruce D.

1995   The Analysis of Single-Household Mississippian Settlements. In *Mississippian Communities and Households,* edited by J. D. Rogers and B. D. Smith, pp. 224–249. University of Alabama Press, Tuscaloosa.

Smith, Marvin T.

ca. late   European Artifacts from the Plum Grove Site, 40Wg17. Manuscript on
1970s   file, Department of Anthropology, Valdosta State University, Valdosta, Georgia.

1987   *The Archaeology of Aboriginal Culture Change: Depopulation during the Early Historic Period.* University Press of Florida, Gainesville.

2002   Aboriginal Population Movements in the Postcontact Southeast. In *The Transformation of the Southeastern Indians, 1540–1760,* edited by R. Ethridge and C. Hudson, pp. 3–20. University Press of Mississippi, Jackson.

Smith, Marvin T., Mark Williams, Chester B. DePratter, Marshall Williams, and Mike Harmon

1988   *Archaeological Investigations at Tomassee (38OC186), a Lower Cherokee Town.* Research Manuscript Series 206. Institute of Archaeology and Anthropology, University of South Carolina, Columbia.

Southworth, Scott, Art Schultz, and Danielle Denenny

2005   *Geologic Map of the Great Smoky Mountains National Park Region, Tennessee and North Carolina.* Open file report submitted to the National Park Service. Electronic document, http://pubs.usgs.gov/of/2005/1225/OF05_1225_report.pdf, accessed July 12, 2008.

Stark, Miriam T.

1998   Technical Choices and Social Boundaries in Material Culture Patterning: An Introduction. In *The Archaeology of Social Boundaries,* edited by M. T. Stark, pp. 1–11. Smithsonian Institution Press, Washington, D.C.

Stewart, John
1931 Letter to William Dunlop, April 27, 1690. *South Carolina Historical and*
[1690] *Genealogical Magazine* 32(1):1–33.
Sullivan, Lynne P.
1989 Household, Community, and Society: An Analysis of Mouse Creek Settlements. In *Households and Communities,* edited by S. MacEachern, D. Archer,
and R. Garvin, pp. 317–327. Proceedings of the Chacmool Conference 21.
Archaeological Association of the University of Calgary, Calgary, Canada.
1995 Mississippian Community and Household Organization in Eastern Tennessee. In *Mississippian Communities and Households,* edited by J. D. Rogers and B. D. Smith, pp. 99–123. University of Alabama Press, Tuscaloosa.
Swanton, John R.
1928 *Social Organization and Social Usages of the Indians of the Creek Confederacy.* Bureau of American Ethnology Annual Report 42. Smithsonian Institution, Washington, D.C.
1930 The Kaskinampo Indians and Their Neighbors. *American Anthropologist*
32:405–418.
1998 *Early History of the Creek Indians and Their Neighbors.* University Press of
Florida, Gainesville. Originally published 1922, Bureau of American Ethnology Bulletin 73, Smithsonian Institution Press, Washington, D.C.
Thomas, Cyrus
1894 *Report on the Mound Explorations of the Bureau of Ethnology.* Bureau of
Ethnology Annual Report 12, pp. 3–730. Smithsonian Institution, Washington, D.C.
Timberlake, Henry
2001 Memoirs. In *The Memoirs of Lieutenant Henry Timberlake,* edited by S. C.
[1762] Williams, pp. 22–175. Mountain Press, Signal Mountain, Tennessee.
Tukey, John W.
1977 *Exploratory Data Analysis.* Addison-Wesley, Reading, Massachusetts.
Turbyfill, Charles O.
1927 Work Done in Western North Carolina during the Summer of 1926. Manuscript on file, Archives of the National Museum of the American Indian,
Washington, D.C.
Usner, Daniel, Jr.
1992 *Indians, Settlers, and Slaves in a Frontier Exchange Economy.* University of
North Carolina Press, Chapel Hill.
van der Leeuw, Sander
1993 Giving the Potter a Choice. In *Technological Choices: Transformation in
Material Cultures since the Neolithic,* edited by P. Lemonnier, pp. 238–288.
Routledge, London.
VanDerwarker, Amber M., and Kandace R. Detwiler
2000 Plant and Animal Subsistence at the Coweeta Creek Site, Macon County,
North Carolina. *North Carolina Archaeology* 49:59–77.

2002   Gendered Practice in Cherokee Foodways: A Spatial Analysis of Plant Remains from the Coweeta Creek Site. *Southeastern Archaeology* 21:21–28.

Varnod, Francis

1971   A True and Exact Account of the Number of Names of All the Towns Be-
[1721] longing to the Cherrikee Nation. In *The Ohio Valley in Colonial Days,* edited by B. Fernow, pp. 273–275. Burt Franklin, New York.

Velleman, Paul F., and David C. Hoaglin

1981   *Applications, Basics, and Computing of Exploratory Data Analysis.* Duxbury Press, Boston.

Walker, Renee B.

1995   Faunal Remains from the Chattooga Site (38Oc18), Oconee County, South Carolina. Manuscript on file, Department of Anthropology, University of Tennessee, Knoxville.

Ward, H. Trawick

1985   Social Implications of Storage and Disposal Patterns. In *Structure and Process in Southeastern Archaeology,* edited by R. S. Dickens Jr. and H. T. Ward, pp. 82–101. University of Alabama Press, Tuscaloosa.

Ward, H. Trawick, and R. P. Stephen Davis Jr.

1991   The Impact of Old World Diseases on the Native Inhabitants of the North Carolina Piedmont. *Archaeology of Eastern North America* 19:171–181.

1999   *Time Before History: The Archaeology of North Carolina.* University of North Carolina Press, Chapel Hill.

2001   Tribes and Traders: Contact and Change on the North Carolina Piedmont. In *Societies in Eclipse: Eastern North America at the Dawn of Civilization,* edited by D. Brose and R. Mainfort, pp. 125–142. Smithsonian Institution Press, Washington, D.C.

Warrick, Gary A.

1988   Estimating Ontario Iroquoian Village Duration. *Man in the Northeast* 36: 21–60.

Waselkov, Gregory A.

1989   Seventeenth-Century Trade in the Colonial Southeast. *Southeastern Archaeology* 8:117–133.

1990   Historic Creek Architectural Adaptations to the Deerskin Trade. In *Archaeological Excavations at the Early Historic Creek Indian Town of Fusihatchee (Phase 1, 1988–1989),* by G. A. Waselkov, J. W. Cottier, and C. T. Sheldon Jr., pp. 39–44. Report submitted to the National Science Foundation, Washington, D.C.

1993   Historic Creek Indian Responses to European Trade and the Rise of Political Factions. In *Ethnohistory and Archaeology: Approaches to Postcontact Change in the Americas,* edited by J. D. Rogers and S. M. Wilson, pp. 123–131. Plenum Press, New York.

1994   The Macon Trading House and Early European-Indian Contact in the Colonial Southeast. In *Ocmulgee Archaeology, 1936–1986,* edited by D. J. Hally, pp. 190–196. University of Georgia Press, Athens.

1998 The Eighteenth-Century Anglo-Indian Trade in Southeastern North America. In *New Faces of the Fur Trade: Selected Papers from the Seventh North American Fur Trade Conference, Halifax, Nova Scotia, 1995,* edited by J. Fiske, S. Sleeper Smith, and W. Wicken, pp. 193–222. Michigan State University Press, East Lansing.

Watanabe, John M.
1992 *Maya Saints and Souls in a Changing World.* University of Texas Press, Austin.

Webb, William S.
1939 *An Archaeological Survey of the Wheeler Basin on the Tennessee River in Northern Alabama.* Bureau of American Ethnology Bulletin 122. Smithsonian Institution, Washington, D.C.

Webb, William S., and David L. DeJarnette
1942 *An Archaeological Survey of Pickwick Basin in Adjacent Portions of the States of Alabama, Mississippi, and Tennessee.* Bureau of American Ethnology Bulletin 129. Smithsonian Institution, Washington, D.C.

Wesson, Cameron B.
1999 Chiefly Power and Food Storage in Southeastern North America. *World Archaeology* 31:145–164.

2008 *Households and Hegemony: Early Creek Prestige Goods, Symbolic Capital, and Social Power.* University of Nebraska Press, Lincoln.

Wilk, Richard R., and Robert McC. Netting
1984 Households: Changing Forms and Function. In *Households: Comparative and Historical Studies of the Domestic Group,* edited by R. McC. Netting, R. R. Wilk, and E. J. Arnould, pp. 1–28. University of California Press, Berkeley.

Wilk, Richard R., and William L. Rathje
1982 Household Archaeology. *American Behavioral Scientist* 25(6):617–640.

Williams, Samuel C. (editor)
1928 *Early Travels in the Tennessee Country, 1540–1800.* Watauga Press, Johnson City, Tennessee.

Wilson, Gregory D.
2005 Between Plaza and Palisade: Household and Community Organization at Early Moundville. Unpublished Ph.D. dissertation, Department of Anthropology, University of North Carolina, Chapel Hill.

2008 *The Archaeology of Everyday Life at Early Moundville.* University of Alabama Press, Tuscaloosa.

Wilson, Gregory D., and Christopher B. Rodning
2002 Boiling, Baking, and Pottery Breaking: A Functional Analysis of Ceramic Vessels from Coweeta Creek. *Southeastern Archaeology* 21:29–35.

Wolf, Eric R.
1982 *Europe and the People Without History.* University of California Press, Berkeley.

Wood, Peter H.
1989 The Changing Population of the Colonial South: An Overview by Race and Region, 1685–1790. In *Powhatan's Mantle: Indians in the Colonial South-*

east, edited by P. H. Wood, G. A. Waselkov, and M. T. Hatley, pp. 35–103. University of Nebraska Press, Lincoln.

Woodward, Henry

1911   A Faithful Relation of My Westoe Voyage. In *Narratives of Early Carolina,*
[1674]   *1650–1708,* edited by A. S. Salley Jr., pp. 125–134. Charles Scribner's Sons, New York.

Worth, John E.

1995   *The Struggle for the Georgia Coast: An Eighteenth-Century Spanish Retrospective on Guale and Mocama.* Anthropological Papers 75. American Museum of Natural History, New York.

2006   Bridging Prehistory and History in the Southeast: Evaluating the Utility of the Acculturation Concept. In *Light on the Path: The Anthropology and History of the Southeastern Indians,* edited by T. J. Pluckhahn and R. Ethridge, pp. 196–206. University of Alabama Press, Tuscaloosa.

Yaeger, Jason, and Marcello A. Canuto

2000   Introducing an Archaeology of Communities. In *The Archaeology of Communities: A New World Perspective,* edited by M. A. Canuto and J. Yaeger, pp. 1–15. Routledge, New York.

Index